D1541580

Separation of
Church and State

דתא·דינא

Judaic Studies Series

Leon J. Weinberger, General Editor

Separation of Church and State

Dina de-Malkhuta Dina
in Jewish Law, 1750–1848

Gil Graff

The University of Alabama Press

Library of Congress Cataloging in Publication Data

Graff, Gil.
   Separation of church and state.
   (Judaic studies series)
   Bibliography: p.
   Includes index.
   1. Judaism and state. 2. Jews—Emancipation.
I. Title. II. Title: Dina de-malkhuta dina.
III. Series.
BM538.S7G73 1985   296.3'877   84-24061
ISBN 0-8173-0264-6

Contents

Contents

Preface

This book examines the changing dimensions of the Jews' relationship to the state in western and central Europe during the eighteenth and early nineteenth centuries. It does so by tracing the Talmudic dictum *dina de-malkhuta dina*, "the law of the kingdom is law," from its classical usage to its expansion to include positive law in addition to "good old law" in the later Middle Ages and, ultimately, to the radical reinterpretation of its scope to incorporate the law of the state in areas that had traditionally been seen as matters exclusively for Jewish legal regulation. The discussions and debates between traditionalists and reformers on the scope of *dina de-malkhuta dina* during the period 1750–1848 reflect the legacy of competing approaches to Jewish accommodation and adjustment to modern Western society bequeathed to Jews of the twentieth century.

The guidance and support of numerous individuals and institutions have made the publication of this work possible. I am grateful to the Lady Davis Fellowship Trust in Jerusalem, the Charlotte Newcombe Fellowship

vii

administered by the Woodrow Wilson Fellowship Foundation, the Sir Simon Marks Fellowship of the Los Angeles Jewish Federation Council's Jewish Community Foundation, the National Foundation for Jewish Culture, and the Department of History at the University of California at Los Angeles, each of which generously provided me with funds for study and research during various stages of this project. The funds provided by the first three of these foundations enabled me to work at libraries and archives in Israel, to the staffs of which research institutes I am indebted. I express my thanks to the librarians of the Judaica Department of the Lady Davis National and University Library in Jerusalem, the archivists at the Central Archives for the History of the Jewish People, particularly to Dr. Simon Schwarzfuchs, whose own work and enthusiastic help were a source of inspiration and encouragement, and to the staff of the Responsa Computer Project at Bar Ilan University.

I am deeply appreciative of the direction and counsel of the many distinguished scholars with whom it has been my pleasure to study during the past decade. Prominent among them are Arnold Band of the UCLA Department of Comparative Literature, David Lieber, president and professor of Bible at the University of Judaism, and Nathaniel Stampfer, chairman of the Department of Education at Spertus College of Judaica. I am particularly indebted to Professor Band for guiding my reading in the Hebrew literature of the *haskalah* and for his close reading of and suggestions regarding earlier drafts of this book.

My greatest scholarly debt, which I gratefully acknowledge, is to Amos Funkenstein. Professor Funkenstein, who divides his academic time between UCLA and Tel Aviv University and between Jewish history and the history of science, is, by his teaching and by his example, a unique inspiration to his students in both universities and in both fields. He first set me to researching *dina de-malkhuta dina*, the "church-state" principle in Jewish law, and directed my attention to the changing dimensions of the principle in medieval and modern times. Demanding but always genial, a mentor and a friend, Professor Funkenstein has been a constant source of insight and assistance throughout the course of my graduate study and to the present.

Beyond acknowledging all of the academic and financial help which I have enjoyed, I thank my parents, who first introduced me to the study of Jewish texts, and express my deep affection and appreciation to my wife Robin, whose patience and understanding during the course of this project have been a source of strength and support. Finally, I thank my sons Ariel and Ilan, whose conversation and cooing, respectively, have helped their father maintain perspective and good cheer during the completion of this work. It is my hope that they will, in their adulthood, be fully conversant with the meaning of *dina de-malkhuta dina*. For the loss of paternal attention sustained during the time this book was written, I express my apology and the happy assurance of remediation.

I am indebted to the editors and publishers of The University of Alabama Press, who have been most gracious and helpful in the process of bringing my manuscript to publication. For the final product of these efforts I assume full responsibility and hope that the reader will find the text both interesting and informative.

Separation of
Church and State

Introduction

Throughout the two and one-half millennia that have passed since the end of the first Jewish commonwealth (586 B.C.E.), Jews and Judaism have confronted the challenge of balancing the demands of religious law with the sometimes conflicting demands of the ruling power. In the spirit of accommodation to the law of the state, Jeremiah counseled the Judeans exiled to Babylonia to "seek the peace of the city whither I have caused you to be carried away captive, and pray unto the Lord for it; for in the peace thereof shall ye have peace."[1] Similarly, Nehemiah advised the Judeans living under Persian rule to accommodate themselves to their subjugation, for God had willed that their overlords "have power over our bodies, and over our cattle, at their pleasure."[2] Little more than one century after Judea had fallen to the Romans (66–73 C.E.), the first-generation *tanna*, Rabbi Ḥanina, declared: "Pray for the welfare of the government, for were it not for the fear of it, men would swallow each other alive."[3]

Not until early in the third century, however, was a

legal principle addressing the issue of the Jews' relationship to state law formulated. In the three words *dina de-malkhuta dina,* "the law of the kingdom is law," the Babylonian *amora,* Samuel, enunciated a doctrine that was to become the basis for defining church-state relations in Jewish law.[4] There are but four references to the principle in the Talmud, none of which sets forth a legal foundation for the dictum.[5]

As did Babylonian Jewry, the European Jewish communities of the Middle Ages enjoyed substantial control over the conduct of their legal affairs. As long as Jews exercised such autonomy, the principle *dina de-malkhuta dina* remained limited in the scope of its application; it was invoked primarily in the realms of taxation, confiscation, and the execution of bills in non-Jewish courts. Its application was defined by rabbinic authorities. The principle not only served as a means of accommodation to the will of the monarch, but it was interpreted so as to provide a legal basis for resistance to the arbitrary demands of the ruling power.

With the erosion of the corporate society of medieval Europe and the emergence of the modern state, the legal autonomy enjoyed by Jewish communities since the initial formulation of Samuel's dictum came to an end. Starting in the eighteenth century, the state increasingly encroached on domains previously reserved to the exclusive jurisdiction of the church. In this new historical milieu, the principle *dina de-malkhuta dina* took on a more expansive role, providing the legal framework for Jewish accommodation to modern Western society. Debate over the extent of *dina de-malkhuta dina* reached its apex in western Europe during the period 1750–1848. Thorough examination of the application and extension of the principle during this century is critical both to an understanding of the Jewish concept of the relationship of its own law to the law of the state and to developing a broader perspective of the process of Jewish accommodation to Western society.

In recent years, two books about *dina de-malkhuta dina* have appeared. The first, Leo Landman's *Jewish Law in the Diaspora: Confrontation and Accommodation* (1968), traces the application of the principle through the Middle Ages and early modern period and concludes with a cursory chapter on "modern questions of *dina de-malkhuta dina*." The more recent work, Shmuel Shilo's *Dina De-Malkhuta Dina* (1974), provides an exhaustive look at the evolving interpretation of Samuel's dictum but does not treat the subject of my study for two reasons: first, the author limited the scope of his work to "normative" Jewish legal currents and did not examine the attempts of nineteenth-century reformers to extend the principle beyond its well-established bounds;[6] and second, the book focuses primarily on the legal issues surrounding interpretation of the dictum, with less attention to the historical circumstances and currents of thought prevailing in each era of its application.[7] Similarly, although numerous excellent historical works have treated the period herein examined, their focus has been limited to social, political, and economic issues, with little systematic attention devoted to the Jewish legal response to the demands of the modern state.[8]

The difficulty of precisely periodizing Jewish history which confronts all historians poses, as well, a problem for delimiting the scope of the present study.[9] Although the corporate existence of European Jewry remained everywhere intact until the closing decade of the eighteenth century, signs of erosion within the Jewish

Introduction

corporate structure were already in evidence in the previous century.[10] In explaining his periodization of Jewish history, according to which the modern period
opens in the middle of the seventeenth century, Salo
Baron observes:

> The Jewish Emancipation era has often been dated from
> the formal pronunciamentos of Jewish equality of rights
> by the French Revolution, or, somewhat more obliquely,
> by the American Constitution. However, departing from
> this purely legalistic approach, I have long felt that the
> underlying more decisive socioeconomic and cultural
> transformations accompanying the rise of modern cap-
> italism, the rapid growth of Western populations, the
> international migrations, the aftereffects of Humanism,
> the Reformation, and the progress of modern science,
> long antedated these formal constitutional fiats. While
> such developments can never be so precisely dated as
> legal enactments, treaties, wars, or biographies of lead-
> ing personalities, the mid-seventeenth century may in-
> deed be considered a major turning point in both world
> and Jewish history.[11]

The aggregate of causes cited by Baron as having con-
tributed to the onset of modernity played an important
role in the trend toward the centralization of state authority which developed at that time. This process of
centralization was to function as the chief external force
eroding Jewish corporate existence and demanding a
redefinition of church-state relations. This process was
well under way by the mid-eighteenth century. The
charter decreed by Frederick II for the Jews of Prussia in
1750 is a significant symbol of the changing relationship
between the Jews and the state. This external symbol of
change serves as one basis for beginning this study in
1750.

4

Introduction

Concomitant with the developing trend toward state centralization was the beginning of the western European Enlightenment, which posited a common capacity of reason, encompassing and uniting all humankind. Enlightened intellectuals raised the issue of extending equal rights to the Jews and generated an internal stimulus toward abdicating traditional norms among segments of Jewish society. The attempt to reconcile Jewish tradition and Enlightenment ideals was most prominently symbolized by Moses Mendelssohn, who, coincidentally, reached his majority in 1750. This year, therefore, takes on a second significance in a study of the changing relationship between religious law and the law of the state in western European Jewish life because it represents a turning point in the process of internal, corporate erosion. It must be emphasized, of course, that both the charter of Frederick the Great and the adulthood of the Maskil ("enlightened") Moses Mendelssohn are symbols of ongoing developments, and the year 1750 therefore serves merely as a convenient benchmark for delimiting the scope of this analysis.

The geographic scope of the present study is limited to western and central Europe, for it was in the German states, the Austrian Empire, and France that the erosion of Jewish community life and the Jews' assimilation to European society accelerated during the eighteenth century. This process was not to affect eastern European Jewry until the following century.

The French Revolution initiated equality of citizenship for the Jews. Not until the reign of Napoleon, however, was the issue of defining the Jews' relationship to the state from the perspective of Jewish law brought to a head. With his flair for classical usages, Napoleon summoned a Grand Sanhedrin, charged with rendering definitive pronouncements on the primacy of the Jews' identity and responsibilities as citizens.

The doctrinal decisions of the Paris Sanhedrin, which began by distinguishing between civil and religious law, were to be variously understood and applied in the decades ahead. Among traditionalists, the civil-religious distinction meant a reaffirmation of the religious basis for the authority of *dina de-malkhuta dina* and of the traditional limitations on the scope of its application. For Jewish religious reformers, who, particularly in the German states, struggled for political and social integration in the generation after Napoleon, the civil-religious distinction meant a total confessionalization of Judaism. Judaism, like Protestantism and Catholicism, was to be a religious creed with no national component. The Jew's sole national loyalty was to the state in which he dwelled. The state would be the ultimate determinant of what was civil and what was religious.

Between these two poles, a variety of approaches to the challenge of Jewish accommodation to modern Western society emerged, each of which has left a continuing legacy. By the time of the 1848 revolutions, all of these positions had been articulated, and discussion of the scope of *dina de-malkhuta dina* in the new age had reached its zenith.

Although the main focus of this study is the use of *dina de-malkhuta dina* during the period 1750–1848, a review of the principle's development before 1750 is critical to an understanding of the controversy that surrounded its application in the modern era. Traditionalist rabbis of any age regard themselves as bound by the legal precedent established by earlier rabbinic authorities. Hence the rabbis of the third century speak to the rabbis of the eighteenth century in a manner that cannot be ignored by the student of Jewish legal history. Further, examining the historical context in which the principle *dina de-malkhuta dina* developed during more than a millennium underscores the radical change in circumstances that confronted the rabbinic authorities of the modern period.

Reflecting these currents, this study is divided into five primary sections. Chapter 1 treats the history of the principle *dina de-malkhuta dina* as it was interpreted and applied from the third to the eighteenth centuries. Chapter 2 explores the changing dimensions of the Jews' relationship to the state under the impact of the Enlightenment and state centralization in western Europe during the latter part of the eighteenth century. Chapter 3 examines the conditions of Jewish life in France at the time of the Revolution. Chapter 4 analyzes the Napoleonic phase in the evolving definition of *dina de-malkhuta dina*. Chapter 5 turns to the role of *dina de-malkhuta dina* in the movement for Jewish religious reform in Germany from 1815 to 1848. A summary and conclusions appear at the end of the work.

In transliterating the various Hebrews terms and titles that appear throughout this text, the abbreviations and transliteration rules set forth in the Index volume of the *Encyclopedia Judaica* (1972) have generally been followed. Talmudic passages rendered in English translation are quoted from the Soncino translation of the Talmud. All Talmudic references are to the Babylonian Talmud unless otherwise indicated.

1. From Talmudic Times to the Eighteenth Century

There are but four references to the dictum *dina de-malkhuta dina* in the Talmud. The discussions in which the principle is mentioned affirm the ruler's authority to collect customs,[1] appropriate palm trees for the construction of bridges,[2] require written deeds of sale to effectuate land transfers,[3] confiscate and sell land for failure to pay the land tax,[4] and ordain that forty years' unchallenged occupancy of land will establish an impregnable claim of ownership.[5] Samuel's statement is also brought in his name to afford legal recognition to bills executed by non-Jewish courts, with the specific exclusion of divorce and manumission.[6]

The authority of the sovereign to collect taxes continued to be a major focus in the application of *dina de-malkhuta dina* when Persian rule gave way to Islamic control. As a result of the Arab conquests of the seventh century, 90 percent of the world Jewish population lived within a single empire. The exilarch, who functioned as the political head of the Jewish community, was recognized as an officer of the caliph. The responsa of the

Gaonic period, which addressed the issue of *dina de-malkhuta*, generally dealt with the limits of the king's taxation authority, which sometimes reached extortionate proportions.[7]

In Christian medieval Europe, the principle *dina-de-malkhuta dina* took on much greater significance. Here, enclaves of Jews living as tolerated corporations in a hostile environment developed a community organization equipped to meet internal needs and to negotiate with external powers for protection.[8] The *kehillah* was governed by a council of annually elected *parnassim*, typically seven in number, and communal life was regulated by *takkanot* (ordinances). When the *parnassim* had adopted an ordinance, with the approval of a recognized rabbinic authority, the *takkanah* would be publicly proclaimed. Unless a formal protest was lodged immediately, the enactment was assumed to have been accepted by general agreement, and every individual became liable to the penalties stipulated for its infraction. Communal leadership was exercised by a hierarchy based upon wealth and scholarship. A measure of regional unity was fostered by the convocation of rabbinical synods, attended by representatives of many *kehillot*, which formulated *takkanot* commonly accepted by the participating communities.[9]

From early in the ninth century, European Jewry lived under various charters modeled on that of Emperor Louis the Pious (son of Charlemagne), which granted them permission "to live according to their law."[10] The charter issued by Emperor Henry IV in 1090, confirming the rights of the Jews of Speyer, typifies the scope of the Jews' medieval corporate privileges. It provides:

1. Henceforth, no one who is invested in our Kingdom with any dignity or power, neither small nor great,

neither free man nor serf, shall presume to attack or assail them on any illicit ground;

2. Nor shall anyone dare to take from them any of their property which they possess by hereditary right. . . .

3. They may have the free right to exchange their goods in just trading with all men and to travel freely in order to carry on their business and trade, to buy, and to sell. No one may exact from them tolls or demand any public or private levy. . . .

6. No one shall presume to baptize their sons or daughters against their will.

13. If the Jews have a dispute or a case among themselves to be decided, they shall be judged and convicted by their peers and by none other.[11]

The terms of this charter reflect the utilitarian nature of the relationship between the emperor and the Jews. The Jews' business activity was protected by the emperor because it represented an important source of revenue through royal taxation.[12] The Jewish community sought the emperor's protection from the hostility of the church and for the exercise of judicial autonomy as necessities for carrying on business life. Although rabbinic authorities viewed their Jewish legal interpretations as the ultimate law of the Jews, the kings of Europe never relinquished their authority to act as the ultimate power in matters affecting their Jews. Thus, from the Jewish viewpoint, *dina de-malkhuta dina* was a limited recognition of "foreign" law based upon the authority of Jewish law, whereas to the medieval king, the law of the land governed the Jews though it accorded them a significant measure of autonomy.

The Talmud is silent as to the legal foundation of the dictum *dina de-malkhuta dina*, and this issue did not engage the attention of the *geonim*.[13] During the medieval period, however, a number of bases for the principle were proposed. Rashi (1040–1105) predicated Samuel's statement on the commandment obligating non-Jews to enact laws to preserve social order. Although all mankind ("the sons of Noah") was obligated to maintain order in the world, the nations of the world were not expected to observe the strictures of Jewish marriage and divorce law. Hence the specific exclusion of writs of divorce from the jurisdiction of non-Jewish courts is readily understood.[14] Other scholars viewed the principle as a matter of implicit, contractual agreement between the king and his subjects. Thus Maimonides (1135–1204), in codifying the law that the principle applies to the edicts of a king whose sovereignty is demonstrated by the circulation of his coins as common, local currency, avers that such usage serves to indicate that the inhabitants of that country have accepted him and take it for granted that he is their master and they are servants to him.[15] Similarly, Rashi's grandson, R. Samuel b. Meir (1085–1174), commented: "For all the citizens accept the king's statutes and laws of their own free will."[16] Rabbi Nissim of Gerondi (ca. 1310–75) explained the contractual basis of *dina de-malkhuta dina* more starkly: because the king owns the land, the Jews are obligated to obey the conditions he establishes for residence thereon.[17] Yet another basis for the contract was the principle that a king acquires total sovereignty over his subjects through military conquest.[18] A third rationale for *dina de-malkhuta dina* was first put forward by Rabbi Ya'akov Tam (ca. 1100–1171), younger brother of the Rashbam (Rabbi Samuel b. Meir). Rabbenu Tam based the rule on the right of the court to uproot a law of the Torah in matters of civil law, *hefker bet din hefker*.[19]

Under such a view, recognition of the statutes of the kingdom by the rabbis was a legitimate exercise of this well-established rabbinic authority.[20] Another view analogized the authority of the ruler to the power of a king of Israel.[21] A fifth view based the legal underpinning of the principle on the *halakhic* validity of customary law.[22] It is no wonder that one of the later authorities observed: "There is great confusion among the legal authorities in this matter [*dina de-malkhuta dina*], and many contradictions . . . I have not seen anyone of the authors who has said something clear and with solid foundation."[23]

The principle, as it was applied, was by no means absolute. The definition of its scope was a matter of ongoing discussion among the *rishonim*[24] and, later, among the *aḥaronim*.[25] A fundamental principle, upon which all authorities agreed, was that *dina de-malkhuta dina* recognition was extended only in monetary matters and not to religious ritual prohibitions *(issur ve-hetter)*.[26] In matters with both monetary and religious aspects, the scope of *dina de-malkhuta* was limited to the commercial dimension. Thus, for example, although marriage was considered a religious act, a government ordinance regulating the amount of a *ketubbah* (marriage contract) payment would be sanctioned under the principle *dina de-malkhuta dina*.[27] Another universally accepted axiom was that the law of the kingdom must apply equally to all the kingdom's inhabitants.[28] But if a law fell equally upon all Jews, even though it was discriminatory against Jews as a class, it was, at times, upheld.[29] This qualification reflected the feudal realities of European Jewish life; the principle was not so qualified by the rabbinic authorities living under Moslem rule.[30]

12

In the spirit of medieval jurisprudence, most of the *rishonim* limited the application of *dina de-malkhuta dina* to ancient law, excluding new legislation enacted by the king.[31] In his incisive article, "Law and Constitution in the Middle Ages," Fritz Kern demonstrates that, during the early Middle Ages, law was a transcendent entity. The power of the state was secondary to and derivative from customary law.[32] Within this context, one rationale for the rabbis' exclusion of positive law from the scope of *dina de-malkhuta* was that the dictum referred to the law of the "kingdom," not to the law of the king.[33] Kern points out that "the Middle Ages knew no genuine legislation by the State. The ordinances or laws of the state aim only at the restoration and execution of valid folk and customary law."[34] Reflective of this attitude is the second basis for limiting the scope of *dina de-malkhuta dina* to ancient legal traditions: as the kings of Israel were restricted in their legislative authority, so were kings of the "nations of the world" bound by ancient law and prohibited from legislating beyond those bounds. Moreover, the very text which enunciated the principle *dina de-malkhuta dina*, BB 55a, seemed to limit the king's authority to alter existing practice through legislation. The Talmud had restricted the king's right to confiscate land to failure to pay the land tax; confiscation for failure to pay the poll tax was specifically excluded. Hence it could be inferred that even if the king desired to confiscate land for failure to pay the poll tax, such a decree would not be accorded recognition under the principle *dina de-malkhuta dina*.[35]

With the developing trend toward the recognition of positive law in the later Middle Ages, changes in the *halakhic* (Jewish legal) position with regard to new legislation became evident. Although the great weight of early *halakhic* authority held that *dina de-malkhuta dina* applied only to ancient law, this view was not shared by Maimonides or by the Rosh (R. Asher ben Yeḥiel, ca. 1250–1327). Consequently, Joseph Caro (1488–1575), codifier of the *Shulkhan Arukh*, who decided the law in conformity with majority rulings between Maimonides, Asher ben Yeḥiel, and Isaac ben Jacob Alfasi (1013–1103),[36] made no mention of the restriction of *dina de-malkhuta dina* to ancient law. Caro's decision to omit this restriction served as a basis for later authorities to extend the principle to the changed concept of legislation in modern times.[37]

Another qualification of *dina de-malkhuta dina* was that the law at issue had been enacted by the bona fide sovereign of the land. Use of the ruler's coins in the territory would evidence the contractual relationship between the sovereign and his subjects.[38]

The king's right to exact the payment of taxes was recognized in the Talmud, and post-Talmudic authorities held that tax evasion was robbery.[39] The Talmud, however, had qualified the right of taxation to assessments bounded by a legally prescribed limit.[40] This qualification served as the basis for the later distinction between legally warranted taxes (those within the scope of *dina de-malkhuta dina*) and taxes considered *gezelah de-malkhuta* (literally, "robbery by the kingdom") and, hence, avoidable.[41] By the fifteenth century, however, a flexible approach was, of necessity, taken in demarcating the limits of legitimate taxation.[42] Similarly, the specific restriction of land confiscation to cases of land tax deliquency, as distinct from failure to pay the poll tax, was swept aside.[43]

To the extent that the concept *gezelah de-malkhuta*

was invoked, it was, of course, no deterrent to the exercise of royal authority. As Salo Baron has observed: "Clearly, under the then existing power relationships, no king treated such rabbinic qualifications as serious obstacles in the enforcement of his decrees."[44] A rabbinic declaration that an act was *gezelah*, however, had significant implications within the Jewish community. If property were stolen, one who later came into its possession would not be considered the rightful owner. A Jew could not benefit from the unlawful confiscation of another Jew's property.[45] To this extent, the principle *dina de-malkhuta dina* was not only one of accommodation but also one of resistance.

It was an accepted axiom of early medieval law that the monarch could not arbitrarily interfere with the well-established rights of the governed; each individual was to be maintained in his existing legal position. This legal conception, rooted in the notion of fealty, recognized as a corollary the subject's right of resistance. Thus the author of the *Sachsenspiegel* asserted: "A man must resist his king and his judge, if he does wrong, and must hinder him in every way, even if he be his relative or feudal lord. And he does not thereby break his fealty."[46] By designating "illegal" confiscations as *gezelah* rather than as *dina de-malkhuta*, Jewish law in effect exercised the right of resistance common to the early medieval period.

The fourteenth-century glossator of the *Sachsenspiegel* reflected the influence of Roman law when he emended Eike von Repgow's assertion with the observation that the king who might be resisted was only a provincial king, not the sovereign *rex Romanorum*. Under similar influence and as an outgrowth of the increasing dependence of the Jews upon the king in the later

Middle Ages, the authority of *hurmena de-malka*, royal regulations, became exalted in Jewish law. A sharp distinction was drawn between the royal prerogative *(hurmena de-malka)* and the authority of Gentile judicial tribunals *(arkha'ot shel goyim)*.[47] Concomitantly, there was a diminution in the invocation of the principle *gezelah de-malkhuta*.

A similar pattern of development toward increasing recognition of the king's law under the principle *dina de-malkhuta dina* is discernible in the matter of *mesirah*, turning over an alleged Jewish criminal, subject to the death penalty, for prosecution by the king's agents. Following the opinion of Resh Lakish in the Palestine Talmud, Maimonides had codified: "If the Gentiles said 'give us one of you and we will kill him and, if not, we will kill all of you,' let them all be killed, but do not turn over one Israelite. But if they specify [a particular individual] and say 'give us so-and-so or we will kill all of you' if he warranted death as did Sheva ben Bichri, he is turned over to them."[48] Opinions differed as to which law must establish the guilt of the accused for purposes of applying this ruling. According to Rabbi Menaḥem ha-Mei'iri, the teaching of Resh Lakish applied only to cases in which the criminal was liable to the death penalty by Jewish law.[49] Similarly, the Rosh permitted false testimony under oath to protect a Jew subject to death by foreign law but not under Jewish law.[50] By the seventeenth century, however, Rabbi David ha-Levi maintained that the accused was to be turned over to the king even if he were liable to death by royal law but not by Jewish law.[51] He derived this conclusion from the phrase "guilty as Sheva ben Bichri."[52] Inasmuch as Sheva ben Bichri was declared guilty by royal order, not by Jewish legal process, it followed that a criminal demanded by the king was to be turned over for prosecution. During the emancipatory era, this position was to be reaffirmed by Rabbi Ishmael ha-Cohen.[53]

The issue of the validity of bills executed in non-Jewish courts was a matter of substantial rabbinic discussion during the Middle Ages.[54] In addition to the *mishnah* in Gittin providing for recourse to non-Jewish courts for the limited purpose of executing certain bills, a further *tannaitic* passage absolutely forbade seeking judgment before a non-Jewish tribunal: "It has been taught: R. Tarfon used to say: In any place where you find heathen law courts, even though their law is the same as the Israelite law, you must not resort to them since it says, 'These are the judgments which thou shalt set before them,'[55] that is to say, 'before them' and not before heathens."[56] The Ashkenazic *rishonim* insisted upon the exclusive jurisdiction of rabbinic courts for Jewish litigants,[57] and this provision was successfully solicited from the secular powers in the Jews' corporate charters.

At a synod at Troyes, about 1150, Rabbenu Tam and other authorities, with the assent of a large group of northern French and possibly western German rabbis, decreed:

> 1. We have voted, decreed, ordained and declared under the herem (ban) that no man or woman may bring a fellow-Jew before Gentile courts or exert compulsion on him through Gentiles, whether by a prince or a common man, a ruler or an inferior official, except by mutual agreement made in the presence of proper witnesses.
>
> 2. If the matter accidentally reaches the government or other Gentiles, and in that manner pressure is exerted on a Jew, we have decreed that the man who is aided by the Gentiles shall have saved his fellow from their

17

hands, and shall secure him against the Gentiles . . . and he shall make satisfaction to him and secure him in such manner as the seven elders of the city will ordain. . . .
   3. He shall not intimidate the "seven elders" through the power of Gentile. And because the masters of wicked tongue and informers do their deeds in darkness, we have decreed also excommunication for indirect action unless he satisfy him in accordance with the decision of the "elders" of the city.[58]

The continuing prohibition against recourse to non-Jewish tribunals was not only rooted in the struggle to preserve judicial autonomy but also in a belief that the *arkha'ot* were fundamentally corrupt and unfair. Thus even for purposes of accepting a document drawn in a non-Jewish court as evidence of a sale, Maimonides required that it be established that the judges and witnesses in the court in question did not accept bribes.[59]

The power of rabbinic authorities to promulgate such legislative enactments as those of Troyes had long been recognized and practiced.[60] The legal basis of this authority was attributed to the biblical verse "According to the law which they shall teach thee and according to the judgment which they shall tell thee, thou shalt do, thou shalt not turn aside from the sentence which they shall declare unto thee, to the right hand nor to the left."[61] Such *takkanot* served to deal with situations not specifically addressed by existing law, to erect a "fence around the law" *(syag la-Torah)*, and, at times, to modify the law to meet the needs of the hour. The principle *hefker bet din hefker*[62] and the exigency jurisdiction termed *hora'at sha'ah*[63] were both extensions of this authority.

Another body of legislation was the communal ordinances, *takkanot ha-kahal*, promulgated at the instigation of the community council. As earlier noted, however, the scope of such ordinances was limited by the requirement that a prospective enactment be approved by a rabbinic scholar prior to its promulgation.[64] Although, because of geographic dispersion, *takkanot* of the post-Gaonic period tended to be local, synodal ordinances sometimes achieved widespread currency.

The force of the "ban" or excommunication which was pronounced upon those who violated certain *takkanot* was formidable. In effect, one who was excommunicated was civilly dead. He had no place within the Jewish community, and in the corporate society of medieval Europe, he had no other option, short of conversion to Christianity.

For its part, Christianity, particularly during the centuries of the Crusades, fostered an increasingly demonic image of the Jews. Starting with the blood libel at Norwich in 1144, the Jews were linked ever more closely with the devil, culminating in the accusation that they had conspired to poison the wells of Europe in 1348–49. It was during this period that distinctive Jewish badges and restrictive ghettos became commonplace. In this milieu, under the guise of Christian piety, various rulers expelled their Jewish subjects. Economic motives, however, were also present; almost every expulsion of Jews was accompanied by confiscation of their property. Thus, for example, in connection with the expulsion of Jews from France in 1306, King Philip IV directed the overseers of Jewish affairs in Orleans as follows: "We command you and each of you to have all lands, houses, vineyards and possessions, which the Jews of the said bailliage held as their own at the time of their arrest, sold at public auction for a just price on our behalf. This should be done as quickly as possible."[65]

As the church became more interested in the realities of Jewish and Moslem belief and practice, the "discovery" was made that the Jews were no longer faithful to the Old Testament; they had supplanted its law with that of the Talmud.[66] Accordingly, the church urged that the Talmud be burned. Aroused by the allegations of Nicholas Donin, a convert from Judaism to Christianity, Pope Gregory IX sent a letter to the king of France in 1239 urging him to seize the books of his Jewish subjects and to transmit these texts to the Dominican and Franciscan friars.[67] Following a "trial," the Talmuds so seized were publicly burned. Part and parcel of the campaign against the Talmud was the series of disputations in the thirteenth century at which Jewish scholars were obliged to defend various doctrines or beliefs against the attacks of Catholic clergy. The forced missionary sermon, frequently delivered in the synagogue, also made its appearance during this period.

The alleged distortion of biblical law by the Jews seriously affected the manner in which the Jews were protected by the monarch. Clerical thought held that Christian kings were excused from the obligations of existing law on the condition that they put into practice the divine law preached and expounded by the church. According to Fritz Kern, "It was one of the most imperishable achievements of ecclesiastical jurisprudence to free the executive power of the state from its subjection to customary law."[68] Perhaps the ultimate exercise of this executive power was the series of mass expulsions of Jews from western European lands during the thirteenth to fifteenth centuries.

In the aftermath of the devastation of the Crusades and the Black Plague, and as result of the increasingly hostile circumstances of Jewish life in western Europe, large-scale Jewish emigration to Poland began. Although a powerful, well-coordinated structure of autonomous government was to emerge in Poland, coordinated rabbinic leadership in western Europe declined noticeably. Owing both to external pressures and to the internal weakening of rabbinic authority, the exclusive jurisdiction of Jewish tribunals over cases involving Jews began to erode. In an effort to combat this trend, a synod of the heads of various German Jewish communities gathered at Frankfurt in 1603 decreed:

> It is a common offense among the people of our generation to refuse to obey Jewish law and even to compel opposing litigants to present themselves before secular courts. The result is that the Holy Name is profaned and that the Government and the Judges are provoked at us. We have therefore decided that anyone who sues his neighbor in secular courts shall be compelled to free him from all the charges made against him, even though the courts decided in favor of the plaintiff. A person guilty of taking a case to Gentile courts shall be separated from the community of Israel, shall not be called to the Torah, and shall not be permitted to marry until he repents and frees his fellow from the power of the Gentile courts. If the defendant was compelled to undertake expenditures in order to bring the infraction of this ordinance before the Jewish courts, the offender shall be compelled to bear the expense.[69]

Notwithstanding the forceful tone of the ordinance, the problem it addressed does not appear to have been solved, as evidenced by continuing rabbinic fulminations against recourse to non-Jewish courts throughout the eighteenth century.

In Spain, rabbinic jurisdiction was in some respects more limited than in western Europe, and in other respects it was greater. Most Jewish courts in Spain were empowered to adjudicate criminal cases with the full support of the state's coercive force. Jewish courts used the prisons of the country to compel obedience to their orders.[70] Floggings, fines, imprisonment, excommunication, and, in extreme cases, mutilation or death were among the penalties imposed by the Jewish courts. R. Asher ben Yeḥiel, who had moved to Toledo from Germany, observed: "When I first arrived here, I asked in amazement by what legal right Jews could, today, legally convict anyone to death without a Sanhedrin.[71] In none of the countries that I know of, except here in Spain, do the Jewish courts try cases of capital punishment."[72]

As late as 1432, a series of statutes adopted at Valladolid for the self-regulation of Castilian Jewry provided:

> Any Jew or Jewess defaming another Jew or Jewess in such a way that harm may result to the Jew or Jewess, even though no Gentile is present, shall be fined for each time he or she used defamatory language, 100 maravedis . . . and shall be imprisoned for ten days. . . . If any Jew or Jewess is alleged to have caused the apprehension of another or the seizure of his property by some Gentile man or woman, but the matter is not substantiated by witnesses being merely supported by the weight of circumstantial evidence, the judge shall have the duty with the counsel of the Rabbi, to order the defamer apprehended and punished bodily in accordance with what seems proper to the scholars so far as they may (legally). If the alleged defamation is confirmed by one witness as well as incriminating circumstances, or if he confesses to it, there shall be branded on his brow the word *Malshin* (slanderer). If the crime is proven through the testimony of two witnesses, the defamed shall receive for the first offense one hundred lashes, and be

driven from the city in accordance with the decision of the Rabbi and the judges and the leaders of the city above-mentioned. If he is guilty of a third offense, as established by the testimony of two proper witnesses, the Rabbi of the Court may in accordance with Jewish law, order his death through the judiciary of our lord, the King.[73]

Not only did the kings in western Europe not grant such sweeping criminal jurisdiction to Jewish tribunals, the exercise of such power by Jewish courts was extra-legal vis-à-vis Jewish law. The Talmudic tractate San-hedrin sets exacting standards of criminal procedure and requires that a court of twenty-three expert judges try capital cases. It was, as Rabbi Asher's observations reflects, a well-accepted principle that in the absence of a Sanhedrin rabbinically ordered capital punishment was impossible. By the same token, with the lapse of ordination *(semikhah)* in the fourth century, there was no body competent under Jewish law to decree flagel-lation or to levy any of the biblically prescribed fines.[74]

The rabbis in Spain meted out such punishments un-der the rationale that they were acting under exigency jurisdiction, *hora'at sha'ah*.[75] Precedent for the rabbinic imposition of extralegal punishment appears in both the Babylonian and Palestine Talmud.[76] A classic statement of the principle is found in BT Tractate Yevamot, folio 90b:

Come and hear: R. Eleazar b. Jacob stated, "I heard that even without any Pentateuchal (authority for their rul-ings), Beth din may administer floggings and (death) penalties; not, however, for the purpose of transgressing the words of the Torah but in order to make a fence for the Torah. And it once happened that a man rode on horseback on the Sabbath in the days of the Greeks, and he was brought before Beth din and stoned; not because he deserved this penalty, but because the exigencies of the hour demanded it. And another incident occurred with a man who had intercourse with his wife under a fig tree, and he was brought before Beth din and flogged; not because he deserved such a penalty, but because the exigencies of the hour demanded it!—to safeguard a cause is different."

Thus for the preservation of the law, ordinary legal norms could be suspended.[77]

In addition to the precondition that it be invoked only for the purpose of protecting the Torah, such emergency authority must also be of a temporary nature,[78] aimed at dealing with a specific, critical situation.[79] The notion of *hora'at sha'ah* was often associated with the verse in Psalms, "It is time to act for the Lord: they have broken thy law."[80]

An interesting parallel to the dual system of justice "at law" and by *hora'at sha'ah* is the Anglo-American distinction between law and equity, which prevailed into the nineteenth century. Starting in the eleventh century, the kings of England expanded and enlarged the exercise of royal prerogative power at the expense of the local courts, which had characterized the English judicial system before the Norman conquest. This prerogative power did not derive from the king's role in the feudal hierarchy but, rather, from his role as protector of the weak and dispenser of justice. Resort to the king's writs and the king's justice became commonplace. Writs of justice were issued in the name of the king by the chancery, which was usually headed by an ecclesiastic. These writs and the forms of action by which they were initiated were, in time, rigidly formalized. Redress for claims outside the scope of the traditional legal forms of action could be sought by petition to the king and his council, operating directly under the royal prerogative power. These petitions were generally referred to the chancellor, who would hear the conflicting parties, evaluate the facts, and render and implement a decision. The chancellors developed both substantive and procedural rules to deal with these problems of equity. This dual system of justice, functioning within the same court structure, was adopted by many of the American colonies. The unification of the substantive law and system of pleading for law and equity actions did not occur until the nineteenth century in the United States.[81]

On the more restrictive side of rabbinic jurisdiction in medieval Spain was the royal policy not to relinquish any of the king's prerogatives.[82] Hence Jewish courts had to contend with royal judges in common areas of jurisdiction. On certain occasions, commercial suits would be brought by Jewish litigants before non-Jewish courts after a rabbinic court had ruled against them. To combat this situation, rabbinic authorities attempted religious coercion. A communal ordinance of the thirteenth century declared: "He who brings suit against his neighbor before the Gentile courts, and thereby causes him to suffer financial losses, shall be excommunicated and remain in this state until he shall render full compensation for the loss sustained."[83]

In part, the efforts of the rabbis in both Ashkenazic and Sephardic lands to limit the litigation of disputes between Jews before non-Jewish courts[84] stemmed from a narrow interpretation of the Talmudic passage which provided for recognition of bills executed in such tribunals:

(Git. 10b) Mishnah: All documents which are accepted in heathen courts, even if they that signed them were Gentiles, are valid except writs of divorce and emancipation. . . . Gemara: Our Mishnah lays down a comprehensive rule in which no distinction is made between a sale and a gift. We can understand that the rule should apply to a sale, because the purchaser acquires the object of sale from the moment when he hands over the money in their (the non-Jewish judges) presence, and the document is a mere corroboration; for if they did not hand over the money in their presence, they would not do injury to themselves (their reputation) by drawing up a document of sale for him. But with a gift [it is different]. Through what [does the recipient] obtain possession? Through this document [is it not]? And this document is a mere piece of clay? Said Samuel: The law of the government is law. Or if you prefer, I can reply: Instead of "except writs of divorce" in the Mishnah read "except [documents] like writ of divorce." (I.e., all which in themselves make the transaction effective, such as the record of a gift.)

By accepting the last line of the above-quoted gemara as the proper explication of the mishnah, all documents which intrinsically effectuate the transaction are excluded from recognition. Only documents that give evidence of the transaction come within the scope of the mishnah's recognition of bills executed in non-Jewish courts. Thus Maimonides stipulated that only commercial transactions (specifically, bills of sale and of indebtedness) could be brought before non-Jewish judges.[85]

In the thirteenth century, a broader interpretation of the Talmudic pasage gave wider scope to the authority of the non-Jewish courts. Nahmanides (1194–1270) understood the ostensibly conflicting readings of the mishnah to be, in fact, complementary. According to Nahmanides, the sentence that gives effect to gifts executed before non-Jewish courts refers to courts under the administration of the king. Such tribunals had broad jurisdiction, restricted only by the *mishnah*'s specific exclusion of writs of divorce and of manumission.[86] Courts that did not function under the king's authority (*hurmena de-malka*) did not have such broad jurisdiction; it was to them that the last clause of the *gemara* referred.[87]

In western Europe, the aftermath of the Crusades gave rise to a new definition of the Jews, as "serfs of the King's chamber."[88] This status had been indicated in the charter of the Emperor Frederick I to the Jews of Worms in 1157, the first clause of which proclaimed: "We wish and command by the authority of our royal dignity, in order that they look to us in all matters of justice, that neither bishop nor treasurer nor count nor judge nor anyone . . . presume to deal with them or against them in any affair or exaction related to justice . . . *since they belong to our treasury as it please us.*"[89] The debacle of the Crusades had accentuated the utter dependence of the Jews upon the emperor for protection.

In this milieu, the interpretation of Nahmanides, distinguishing documents executed in royal courts from the tribunals of other authorities, gained increasing recognition. The Rosh (R. Asher ben Yehiel) used Nahmanides' distinction between courts functioning by *hurmena de-malka* and courts not so empowered to interpret the Talmudic passage to hold that when there was a legal requirement to bring documents before non-Jewish courts (understanding "hurmena" to mean "coercion"), documents executed before a non-Jewish tribunal were to be recognized, even if they effectuated a transaction. If, however, it was not required that documents be brought before the non-Jewish court, they were to be recognized only to the extent that they gave evidence of a transaction.[90] Among the *aḥaronim*, this approach became the accepted interpretation of the Talmudic passage. The opinion of the Rosh was recorded as the operative law by Moses Isserles (ca. 1525–72) in his gloss to the *Shulkhan Arukh*.[91]

As H. H. Ben-Sasson has observed, the end of the ideological and practical unity of Western Christendom as a result of the Protestant Reformation in the sixteenth century was to have the ultimate, unintended effect of advancing secularist trends in European society.[92] The Protestant emphasis on the scriptural text gave rise to a more critical reading of the Bible and, in some quarters, to a modicum of respect for the Jews. At very least, the Jews ceased to be the only "heretics" in the kingdoms of Europe.

In the aftermath of the Thirty Years' War (1618–48) in central Europe and the Chmielnicki rebellion in the Ukraine (1648–49), Jewish refugees began to settle in commercial centers that were developing in the West. Concomitantly, rising absolutism was effecting the breakdown of medieval corporate structures. A gradual erosion of traditional Jewish communal authority was already discernible in the century before the legal dissolution of Jewish autonomy.

During the long span of years between the third and eighteenth centuries, there was a remarkable uniformity in the range of issues arising in connection with the definition of *dina de-malkhuta dina*.[93] The applications of the principle cited in the few Talmudic references to it—taxes, confiscations, and bills executed in non-Jewish courts—were the primary issues that arose in its further interpretation during the following one and one-half millennia. That the source of authority for the principle *dina de-malkhuta dina* was Jewish law itself was a fundamental axiom in its rabbinic application. This phenomenon is in large measure attributable to the legal autonomy that characterized Jewish life until the emancipation. Only with the accelerated breakdown of corporate society in the West was the legal basis of *dina de-malkhuta dina* to be reexamined and the scope of its application extended. It is to this period that we now turn.

2. The Impact of the Enlightenment and the Centralization of State Authority

The seventeenth and eighteenth centuries were an era of significant commercial and political change in western Europe. Monarchs vied with one another to accumulate wealth by establishing and exploiting overseas colonies, developing new industries, and exporting goods to distant markets, while, within their respective realms, they struggled to strengthen their authority over corporations and estates in a quest to achieve absolute power.[1] In this milieu, the role of the Jew in society became more highly valued than in medieval times, and Jews became an important tool of monarchial policy. First and foremost, Jews were seen as sources of ready, liquid investment capital.[2] As the most marginal element of European society, the Jew was politically impotent and thus ideally suited to use by the ruling power.

At the apex of this relationship between the Jews and European rulers endeavoring to centralize authority stood the court Jew, who, especially in the German states, emerged as a crucial supplier of munitions and food for the military.[3] Jewish bankers also made their appearance in early modern Europe. Although these *Hofjuden* were small in number, their importance to the reigning authority was often the reason why other Jews were tolerated in the kingdom. Although every German state had its special laws governing the rights of Jewish domicile and regulating occupational pursuits, the eighteenth century saw a steady increase in the number of Jews living amid the non-Jewish population.[4] As individual Jews emerged from their traditional Jewish environment, they began to adopt the outer trappings of European culture and, gradually, to lose touch with the social goals of their co-religionists. At the same time, the absolutist state moved toward disbanding the structure of Jewish autonomy.[5] These two developments, the erosion of traditional values from within Jewish circles and the abolition of traditional privileges on the road to centralized state authority, were to set the stage for a broadened debate over the application of *dina de-malkhuta dina* in the nineteenth century.

Perhaps the most striking area of erosion in Jewish autonomy during this period was the decline of rabbinic court jurisdiction. From without, jurists called for the abolition of Jewish judicial autonomy. As one contemporary writer put it:

> Jews should not be permitted secular jurisdiction and their exercise of judicial authority in resolving disputes ought not to be tolerated. Inasmuch as the Righteous God destroyed the city of Jerusalem and the Land of the Jews and wiped out Jewish sovereignty and gave over the Jews to the rule of the Roman Caesar, it is self-evident that they should not be given new opportunities to adjudicate cases, resolve disputes, to bring fellow Jews to (their) court, to levy taxes, to enter contracts (by their

31

own formulas) or to punish as they wish such wrong-
doers as thieves, murderers or adulterers.[6]

Internally, among the Jews of the German states, there
was increasing disaffection with rabbinic courts and re-
ferral to non-Jewish tribunals.[7]

The charters granted the Jews in the late seventeenth
and early eighteenth centuries substantially eliminated
rabbinic judicial authority in other than ceremonial
and ritual matters. Concomitantly, the power to issue a
ḥerem (excommunication) was severely circumscribed.[8]
The "Revised General Privilege and Regulation for the
Jewry of Prussia," promulgated by Frederick II in 1750,
was clear about these matters:

> Quarrels that occur actually in the synagogue because of
> Jewish ceremonies and synagogal customs are to be dis-
> cussed and settled by the rabbi or vice-rabbi and the
> elders. According to circumstances they themselves
> may fine the offenders with a moderate money penalty.
> However they shall not proceed against any one with the
> ban and money fines that amount to more than five
> *Reichsthalers,* without the previous knowledge of the
> city authorities; such penalties shall not be imposed on
> anyone by the rabbi alone nor even with the elders. He
> shall not presumptuously undertake to make any real
> decision and settlement of a case in matters of secular
> law, for the rabbi and the elders have no right to real
> jurisdiction. On the contrary, matters of law must be
> referred to the proper court of justice. However, in mat-
> ters in which Jews have to do with Jews and which come
> within the province of their rites, such as Jewish mar-
> riage-contracts and their validity in bankruptcy, deter-
> mination of the heir in cases of succession to estates,
> which can only be settled by them through their Mosaic
> laws, we concede, for the present, some sort of legal

jurisdiction to the rabbis and their learned assistant-judges. This also applies to other judicial acts such as wills, inventories, and appointment of guardians. The Jewish jurisdiction, however, is only in the form of arbitration. When the litigants are not satisfied with a decision they always have the privilege of referring their case back to the ordinary judges as a simple judicial case without respect to the statute of limitations. And the rabbis and the assistant-judges are herewith responsible when they do not proceed legally in matters of inventories, divisions of estates, and appointment of guardians.[9]

The charter of Frederick II reflects a gradual change in the place of the Jew in European society not only as an outgrowth of state centralization but in furtherance of mercantilist economic goals. In 1671, Frederick William had admitted to Berlin fifty Jewish families expelled from Vienna by Emperor Leopold I for the stated purpose of furthering business.[10] Similar to the charters of the Middle Ages, the edict of Frederick William assured the Jews protection and the freedom to engage in commerce in return for significant tax revenues. The role of the Jew in the Prussian economy was further articulated by Frederick the Great, when, in turning down the application of a Jew to lease a dairy farm, he said that the Jews were tolerated only for the sake of trade and manufacture but that agriculture was reserved for Christians. The charter of Frederick II and subsequent regulations specifically defined the scope of Jewish business activity. To promote industry, he bestowed the right of settlement upon second-born sons of regular protected Jews, with the proviso that they set up factories. He demanded that Jews give preference to goods manufactured in Prussia and that they sell these wares in Russia,

Poland, Lithuania, Bohemia, Moravia, France, and other German states. The existing prohibition against Jews pursuing manual trades was waived for those establishing certain types of factories.[11]

As the eighteenth century progressed, the influence of the outside culture penetrated the thinking of an element of tolerated Jews living outside the ghetto far more deeply than it had during the previous century.[12] This process was facilitated by the general secularization of society, which enabled Jew and Christian to meet on neutral ground. The philosophy of the Enlightenment, apart from rendering God a probable truth not dependent upon the dogma of historical religion, posited a shared faculty of understanding among men, all of whom were capable of recognizing certain "self-evident" truths. Intellectuals of this period would not allow class or religious distinction to interfere in the common ideals of the Enlightenment. To this group, like-thinking Jews could assimilate without denying their religion.

Notwithstanding the enlightened posture of many such intellectuals, there were those whose devotion to Christian dogma underlay the veneer of the Enlightenment. It is well known that Moses Mendelssohn's turn to Jewish philosophical writing during the last part of his life was sparked by the challenge of the Swiss theologian Johann Caspar Lavater, who urged him publicly either to refute Christianity or to convert to the true faith.[13] Still another challenge was issued, more than a decade after Lavater's, in an anonymous pamphlet titled *The Searcher for Light and Right*, which confronted Mendelssohn with the implications of his stated objection to ecclesiastical authority. If, as the "Searcher" thought, ecclesiastical authority was essential to Judaism, then, he alleged, Mendelssohn had left the faith of his fathers and was but a step removed from Christianity. It was in this historical climate that Mendelssohn wrote his *Jerusalem* (1783).

In *Jerusalem,* Mendelssohn distinguished between "eternal truths," which are self-evident principles of reason, and "divine law," which is God's revealed will: "The Israelites possess a divine legislation—laws, commandments, statutes, rules of conduct, instruction in God's will and in what they are to do to attain temporal and eternal salvation. Moses, in a miraculous and supernatural way, revealed to them these laws and commandments, but not dogmas, propositions concerning salvation, or self-evident principles of reason. These the Lord reveals to us as to all other men at all times through nature and event but never through the spoken or written word."[14] Thus Mendelssohn identified the doctrinal part of Judaism with natural religion. Knowledge of the "eternal truths" was not a matter of supernatural revelation but, rather, a universal heritage, intelligible to all men.

Having defined Judaism as a religion of revealed law, Mendelssohn was constrained to explain the necessity of the "divine precepts." The legal institutions of Israel were accounted by him as stimuli to the contemplation of eternal verities. Natural religion might lapse into superstition and idolatry, but the descendants of Abraham, Isaac, and Jacob were "a nation which, through its constitution and institutions, through its laws and conduct, . . . was to call wholesome and unadulterated ideas of God and His attributes continuously to the attention of the rest of mankind."[15] As for the continuing obligation of the Jew to observe divine law, Mendelssohn distinguished between observances that were symbolic actions and hence eternally valid and laws that were vestiges of Israel's political constitution and thus abrogated upon the loss of national sovereignty.[16]

Mendelssohn's separation of the doctrinal from the legislative component of Judaism was a distinction that had been made a century earlier by Baruch Spinoza, but with radically different conclusions. For Spinoza, natural law, which is Divine law, is universal. The ceremonial aspect of Mosaic law was designed to transform the Hebrew slaves into an obedient body politic, capable of functioning as a state in a particular territory. Therefore, Spinoza concluded, it cannot be doubted "that they (Jews) were no more bound by the law of Moses, after the destruction of their kingdom, than they had been before it had been begun, while they were still living among other peoples before the exodus from Egypt, and were subject to no special law beyond the natural law, and also, doubtless, the law of the state in which they were living, insofar as it was consonant with Divine natural law."[17] Although Mendelssohn took a different view of the ceremonial law, he implicitly removed it from the realm of what Spinoza defined as Divine law: "that which only regards the highest good, in other words, the true knowledge of God and love."[18] If the biblically commanded ceremonies were merely symbols, it was not a great leap to conclude that they were superfluous formalities.

More than being a treatise on religion, however, *Jerusalem* was a statement of Mendelssohn's political philosophy and a delineation of the respective roles of church and state. The state, according to Mendelssohn, is characterized by its coercive power to defend rights and render decisions. This right of coercion springs from the social contract, which arose by the surrender of the individual's natural prerogative to decide cases of competing claims. The church has no right to exercise coercive power, for in matters of man's relationship with God there is no possibility of the collision of competing claims. Only in the ancient Jewish state, in which God was the ultimate sovereign, was a unity of the state and religion proper. The power of religion today lies in teaching and moral suasion. Within this framework, there is no place for excommunication: "The right to banishment and expulsion which the state may occasionally allow itself to exercise is diametrically opposed to the spirit of religion."[19] In denying the power of the church or the synagogue to excommunicate its members, Mendelssohn opposed a fundamental norm of European Jewish life. In effect he challenged the corporate structure of Jewish society.

Mendelssohn's view of the compatibility of Judaism with the modern state was abetted by his readiness to abandon religious custom in the name of reason. This tendency was evidenced in a responsum Mendelssohn wrote on the question of delayed burial of the dead. On April 30, 1772, Duke Friedrich issued an order to his Jewish subjects of Mecklenburg-Schwerin, prohibiting the religious practice of immediate burial and requiring a waiting period of three days to assure that the person to be buried was, indeed, deceased. On May 15, the Jewish community, which was legally protected from interference with Jewish law and custom, petitioned the duke to rescind the order, pending testimony from noted authorities on the issues of Jewish law at question. Among the authorities consulted was Moses Mendelssohn (the other, unbeknownst to Mendelssohn, was Jacob Emden, one of the outstanding rabbinic authorities of the generation). Mendelssohn responded with a letter to the duke, in German, adducing compelling religious bases for the Jewish burial practice and indicating that the Jews of Schwerin would henceforth request a medical certificate of death prior to burial. Mendelssohn also wrote a letter in Hebrew to the leaders of the Schwerin Jewish community, chiding them for their unwillingness to yield on a matter that was, in his view, without solid foundation in Jewish law: "You are pained and saddened concerning this [matter] as though he [the duke], God forbid, wanted to cause transgression of the faith or make you stumble in sin over a biblical or rabbinic prohibition. I cannot fathom what you have seen in this matter and what ominous fear you have with regard thereto." Rabbi Jacob Emden saw great danger in Mendelssohn's private position on this issue. In his view, it signified a willingness "to negate a prohibition of the sages altogether"[21] in order to accommodate to the norms of the environment.

Just as a church could not assume state functions, in Mendelssohn's thinking, so the state was not to impose religious doctrine upon its inhabitants. The right to use coercion, obtained by the state through the social contract, was applicable only to actions, not to sentiments or convictions. Therefore, urged Mendelssohn, "Let every man who does not disturb the public welfare, who obeys the law, acts righteously towards you and his fellowmen be allowed to speak as he thinks, to pray to God after his own fashion or after the fashion of his fathers and to seek eternal salvation where he thinks he may find it."[22] Mendelssohn counseled the Jews to "adopt the mores and constitutions of the country in which you find yourself, but be steadfast in upholding the religion of your fathers, too."[23]

Coincidentally, the appearance of *Jerusalem* followed

by one year the publication of the *Toleranzpatent* by Kaiser Joseph II in Austria. This patent, which encouraged a measure of Jewish integration into the larger society through expanded educational and economic opportunities, was hailed by the *maskilim* ("enlightened") as a momentous advance in the cause of Jewish enlightenment.[24] Naphtali Herz Wessely responded with his manifesto, *Divrei Shalom ve-Emet* (Words of Peace and Truth) addressed to the "Congregation of Israel Which Dwells in the Domain of the Great Kaiser Joseph II, Who Loves and Who Gladdens All Mankind." In this exuberant tract urging Austrian Jewry to comply willingly with the kaiser's order to open schools in which German would be taught, Wessely distinguished between human knowledge *(Torat ha-Adam)* and divine law *(Torat ha-Shem).* Although Jewish education required schooling in both areas, Wessely maintained that the study of human knowledge should precede the study of God's law because the former is a necessary basis for understanding the latter. Implicit in this formulation was the subordination of Judaism to secular knowledge and natural religion.[25]

The issue of education for Jewish youth in the new age was a major topic of discussion in the circle of *maskilim* assembled around Mendelssohn. David Friedlander, aided by Mendelssohn, composed the first German reader for Jewish children, a book filled with the enlightened humanism of the time.[26] The educational motive was also responsible for the *beiurim* (German translation of the Pentateuch, with commentary) of Mendelssohn and his younger contemporaries.[27] Primary themes in the educational writings of the *maskilim* were the brotherhood of man, devotion to the state and government, and the necessity of economic rehabilitation. By educating their coreligionists, the *maskilim* hoped to prepare the way for political emancipation.[28]

The same Joseph II whose *Toleranzpatent* gave the *maskilim* hopes of a new dawn injected the state into the regulation of marriages, through the *Ehepatent* of 1783. Previously this subject had been left to religious jurisdiction. Although it is not within the scope of this study to examine the complex structure of Jewish family law, a brief review of several basic legal principles will provide the background necessary for understanding the impact of this and related phenomena affecting Jewish autonomy during the late eighteenth and early nineteenth centuries. It was in the area of family law, particularly marriage and divorce, that the demands of state law first collided with Jewish religious law in the emancipatory era.[29]

Marriage, in Jewish law, is effectuated in a two-step legal procedure. The first phase, *kiddushin*, also referred to as *erusin*, is an act by which the man "acquires" the affianced woman, establishing a legal relationship that can be terminated only by divorce or by the death of either party.[30] There are three ways of accomplishing *kiddushin: kesef* (money), *shetar* (document), or *biah* (cohabitation).[31] *Kiddushin* by *kesef* is effected by the man's transferring a minimum sum of money or its equivalent to the woman, before two competent witnesses, while reciting a formula proclaiming his intent to establish a marital relationship.[32] *Kiddushin* by *shetar* is accomplished by the man's handing the woman a document recording the names of the parties and the formula of bridal acquisition before two competent witnesses. *Kiddushin* by *biah* is effectuated by the man's declaring to a woman before two competent witnesses: "Behold you are consecrated to me with this cohabitation according to the law of Moses and Israel," and proceeding, in the presence of the witnesses, to take her into a private place. The Talmudic sages frowned upon the last-mentioned mode of *kiddushin,* and they ordained that any person who exercised it would be punished by flogging.[33] At the same time, however, a presumption existed that "no man engages in sexual intercourse for licentious purposes" *(ein adam oseh be-ilato be-ilat zenut),* and cohabitation with an unmarried woman was, therefore, presumably intended to effectuate *kiddushin.* This presumption was rebuttable.[34]

The formula of *kiddushin* "by the law of Moses and Israel" was so interpreted as to establish the rabbis as the ultimate determinants of the validity of the *kiddushin.*[35] Based upon this authority, the Talmudic rabbis assumed the power of annulment in certain cases: *Kol ha-mekadesh a-da'ata de-rabbanan mekadesh ve-afki'inhu rabbanan le-kiddushin minah* (all who marry do so by the authority of the rabbis).[36] Rabbinic annulment was considered possible no matter how the *kiddushin* had been effectuated. If the *kiddushin* was accomplished by money, the rabbis expropriated the money, exercising the power *hefker bet din hefker.*[37] If the *kiddushin* was effected by document, the document was declared ownerless and the relationship based thereon was nullified. As for *kiddushin* by cohabitation, the rabbis declared the intercourse to have been mere license and hence ineffective as a means of establishing *kiddushin.*

In the post-Talmudic period, there was disagreement over the authority of the latter-day rabbis to annul *kiddushin.* Some scholars ruled that because of the gravity of matrimonial matters only a court such as that of Rabbi Ami and Rabbi Ashi, the authority of which was recognized by the entire Jewish people, could exercise expropriative power in this sphere of law and that only a *get* could sever the *kiddushin* relationship.[38] The less restrictive view held that *kiddushin* is always subject to the consent of the sages.[39] Every community could, with the approval of its members and scholars, enact measures regulating *kiddushin* and ordain that the money given by way of *kiddushin* be expropriated, thereby nullifying the *kiddushin*, in the event of a transgression of such community ordinances.[40] Moreover, betrothal by intercourse could be declared mere license and hence ineffectual as *kiddushin*.[41]

Only after the second phase of the marriage process, *nissu'in*, celebrated publicly by the recitation of the "seven benedictions" *(sheva berakhot)*, did the mutual rights and duties of husband and wife become fully vested and the husband become responsible for the maintenance of the bride. The *arus* (affianced man) was not responsible for the maintenance of his bride for a period of twelve months from the time of the *kiddushin*, and the *arusa* (affianced woman) did not, by right, receive a *ketubbah* until the *nissu'in*.[42]

Biblical law provides for a husband's divorcing his wife by issuing a "document of cutting off" *(sefer kritut)*,[43] and Talmudic law details both the substantive and procedural regulation of divorce. Although the divorce is an act between the parties, it is the function of a rabbinic court to direct the course of the proceeding to ensure that the legal formalities required for Jewish divorce are properly carried out.[44] If a Jewish divorce *(get)* is not executed, the spouses remain married in the eyes of Jewish law, and their subsequent marriage is considered bigamy.[45]

Under some circumstances the parties were com-

pelled to divorce, such as when a marriage, though prohibited, was not classified as *gillui arayot* (biblically
prohibited).[46] Included in this category of prohibited-
though-valid marital unions were cases of incest of a
secondary degree and the marriage of a married man to a
second woman before his first marriage has been terminated, in contravention of the *ḥerem de-Rabbenu
Gershom*.[47]

Before the eighteenth century, legal discussions on
the validity of Jewish marriage contracted outside the
above-described framework dealt primarily with marriages entered into according to Christian or Moslem
practice.[48] Such cases frequently arose when the marriage of the parties in a non-Jewish ceremony was followed by the husband's abandonment of the wife and
the wife's subsequent desire to marry according to Jewish law. The legal issue so presented was whether the
woman was to be considered an *agunah*,[49] hence not
permitted to marry, or whether the first union was to be
considered of no legal force. Many such cases arose during periods of persecution and expulsion, particularly
during the Spanish Inquisition.

In the fourteenth century, Isaac ben Sheshet Perfet
(Ribash, 1326–1408) was asked to rule on the validity of
kiddushin in a case in which two Marranos had been
married by a priest and had then lived together three
months, during which period the woman had become
pregnant. The husband went overseas and did not return; if the marriage were to be held valid, the woman
would be an *agunah*. Ribash, in an oft-quoted responsum, ruled that there had been no *kiddushin*.[50] First,
there had been no marriage by money or document because the procedural requirements attendant on such
kiddushin were lacking. Second, there could not have

been *kiddushin* by cohabitation because the formula of *kiddushin* by *biah* had not been pronounced by the husband. The presumption that "no man engages in sexual intercourse for licentious purposes" was inapplicable when the parties clearly indicated that they did not intend to be married by "the law of Moses and Israel."[51] In any event, that principle applied only to law-abiding individuals, not to lawless persons. That these people had been married by a priest attested to their lawless character. In closing, Rabash commented that there was no need to look for stringent rationales by which to make the woman an *agunah*.[52]

A similar case was reported by Rabbi Israel Isserlein (1390–1460) in Germany. Two apostates were married by a priest and lived together for two or three years. Thereafter, the woman returned to Judaism and wanted to marry a Jew. Isserlein permitted the marriage concluding for reasons identical to those of Ribash, that the first union had been "mere license."[53]

The process of Islamic marriage was markedly different from the Catholic ceremony, in the absence of any religious ritual. The couple simply appeared before a judge and transacted a marriage agreement, an act devoid of religious celebration. Although aware of this difference, rabbinic authorities did not distinguish between the legal status of such unions and those entered into within the church. Thus, for example, in a lengthy responsum, Rabbi Mordecai ha-Levi (d. 1684) held that a marriage of two Jews by Islamic procedure, which had lasted several years and produced a child, was not a valid marital union by Jewish law, even though the marriage ceremony involved "no act of withdrawal from the [Jewish] legal framework." Upon the husband's disappearance, the woman was not to be considered an *agunah* "for every man who marries a woman contrary to [Jewish] law but, rather, marries by non-Jewish courts, we do not consider his cohabitation with her [an act of *kiddushin*]."[54] Marriages contracted other than by Jewish law, whether undertaken by Catholic or by Islamic procedure, were consistently held to be without legal standing by rabbinic authorities.[55]

The entry of the state into the regulation of marriage in the eighteenth century added a new dimension to the legal questions raised by marriages contracted outside of Jewish law. Not only was there the old problem of the validity of a marriage ceremony not in keeping with Jewish legal requirements but also the new issue of the validity of *kiddushin* effectuated in contravention of state law. Over this question discussions about the relationship between Jewish and state law were renewed with great vigor.

The first country to provide for civil marriage as an option was Holland, in 1580. At about the same time, Marranos of Spanish and Portuguese origin were beginning to find refuge in Amsterdam. In the course of the seventeenth and eighteenth centuries, Sephardim and, later, Ashkenazim, settled in Holland in growing numbers, establishing separate community organizations. Compared with the situation in other European states, the lot of Dutch Jewry was favorable.[56] The strength of the *kehillot* in Holland during this period is reflected in the fact that the question of civil marriage did not arise until 1741.[57] In that year, we read of a certain Yoḥanan who, having been denied the opportunity of marrying a particular woman by the *parnassim* of her community when it was discovered that he already had a wife in another city, married the woman by the available civil procedure and lived with her for many years.[58]

45

Sometime later, he abandoned the second woman and returned to his first wife, whom he had married by Jewish law. The abandoned woman sought permission from the Jewish court to marry.[59] Citing Ribash, the responsum that addressed this problem held that the union effectuated by the law of the state was of no Jewish legal consequence; hence the woman was free to marry.[60] This responsum clearly placed civil marriage on a par with marriages contracted by Catholic or Moslem practice.

The problem of state-mandated regulation of marriage was first confronted by Austrian Jewry when, in 1783, Kaiser Joseph II promulgated the *Ehepatent*, regulating the marriages of all inhabitants of the empire. Many elements of the Austrian law were patterned on canon law and differed from the framework of Jewish marriage law. Forbidden degrees of relationship were extended beyond biblical strictures, including, for example, the marriage of a man to his niece. Persons under the age of twenty-four were obliged to secure the consent of their father or legal guardian to marry. Forthcoming marriages were to be proclaimed on three consecutive Sabbaths, in the synagogue, and were to be performed only by a state-authorized district rabbi. The ordinance decreed that marriages not in compliance with state law would be considered null and void.[61] The protests of Austrian Jews led Joseph II to solicit the opinion of Rabbi Ezekiel Landau of Prague (1713–93) on the extent, if any, to which the *Ehepatent* collided with Jewish law. Landau responded with a tract titled "Jewish Marriage according to the Law of Moses and the Talmud."[62]

Landau began with some general observations on marriage in Jewish law. He noted that Jewish law did not recognize a marriage of a Jew with other than a Jewish partner and that, once entered, the marital bond could be severed only by death or divorce. Marriage law, observed Landau, was an area of utmost stringency in Jewish law. He then proceeded to a point-by-point discussion of the regulations of the *Ehepatent*. With regard to the list of prohibited marriages which extended beyond the limitations set by Jewish law, he maintained that any such extension of marriage prohibitions was impossible, according to *halakha*.[63] The Deuteronomic proscription against adding to the law included a government ordinance such as the *Ehepatent*.[64] Even the Sanhedrin, wrote Landauu, could not forbid that which was permitted by the Torah.[65] Landau declared that Jewish law stipulated thirteen years as the age of majority for males and twelve years for females. The *kiddushin* of an adult, so defined, would be valid, notwithstanding parental objection. But Landau indicated that the rabbis of the Austrian Empire would endeavor to observe the requirements of publicly announcing upcoming marriages and of securing the authorization of the father of minors, as required by state law. The tone of the tract was clear. The kaiser's Jewish subjects would try to comply with the law of the state, but Jewish law remained paramount: *kiddushin* effectuated by Jewish legal process, though contrary to civil requirements, would not be considered null. Landau closed with a plea that the kaiser not infringe upon the Jews' traditional autonomy: "May His Honored Majesty, the kaiser, in his great mercy, continue to bestow his righteousness upon us in the future as at present, to envelope us 'neath his wings and to protect us in our religious laws and judgments so as to diminish nothing from them nor to move them from their place."[66] Notwithstanding Landau's plea, the terms of the *Ehepatent* were reaffirmed in 1786.[67]

47

A concrete case, emerging out of a failure to comply with provisions of the *Ehepatent*, arose in Trieste, then a part of the Austrian Empire, in 1796. A Jewish man betrothed a Jewish woman who was not yet twenty-four by religiously valid *kiddushin*. This *kiddushin*, however, took place without the consent of the woman's father, who was now protesting, and with neither the state-required proclamations nor the officiation of the authorized district rabbi. The rabbi of Trieste sought the opinion of Rabbi Eliezer Fleckeles (1754–1826) of Prague, successor to Ezekiel Landau as head of the *bet din*, as to the status of this union and how best to proceed. Fleckeles affirmed that if the *kiddushin* had been effected before two competent witnesses it was valid, according to Jewish law. As to the conflict with state law, he averred that it was surely not the intent of Kaiser Joseph II to deny the legality of a union entered into through *kiddushin*: "True and certain it is that it has not dawned upon any king in several generations to terminate any of the mitzvot or to trangress His [God's] Will; to the contrary, all of them are righteous kings, strengthening the religion of each and every nation."[68] Rather, maintained Fleckeles, the *Ehepatent* applied only to *nissu'in*, not to *kiddushin*. If, arguably, *kiddushin* were included in the kaiser's decree, the betrothal would still be effective. This conclusion was drawn by analogy to secondarily prohibited marital unions, which were legally valid, albeit the divorce of the parties was compelled.[69] If the *Ehepatent* had included *kiddushin*, a marriage contracted in contravention of the law would, though valid, have necessitated a *get*, for "one who transgresses the command of the Kaiser Joseph II is as one who transgresses the law of God Almighty."[70]

Because *kiddushin* was not a part of the *Ehepatent*,

according to Fleckeles's reading, Jewish law could not require a divorce. Having transgressed state law with regard to *nissu'in*, however, the couple could not live together as man and wife. Unless and until the woman received a *get*, she would remain an *arusa*. To enable the woman to marry at some future time, counseled Fleckeles, the man should be encouraged to give her a *get*. In the manner of his mentor, Ezekiel Landau, Fleckeles extolled Joseph II as one who "loves righteousness and justice in his lands and desires that they (the inhabitants) all be children of faith and [who] doesn't wish to uproot the religion which was given to any people."[71]

Fleckeles's novel interpretation of the *Ehepatent* left a woman who wed contrary to the law in a worse position than she would have occupied under a more literal understanding of the kaiser's decree. If both *kiddushin* and *nissu'in* were included in the decree, the man would have been obliged by Jewish law to give the woman a *get*. But because *kiddushin* was considered to have been outside the scope of the *Ehepatent*, the execution of a *get* was to be a voluntary act of the *arus*. Although, ostensibly puzzling, Fleckeles's interpretation can be understood as an attempt to assert the primacy of Jewish jurisdiction in matters of family law in the face of state encroachment. First, it affirmed the unrestricted application of Jewish law in effectuating *kiddushin*. Second, by making the issuance of a *get* a voluntary rather than a mandated act, it clearly distinguished between the legal effect of the kaiser's decree and other, more indigenous, prohibitions on marriage within Jewish law, notwithstanding rhetoric to the contrary. The language of Fleckeles's responsum appears more yielding than that of Landau's tract because Landau was writing a treatise aimed at modifying the kaiser's decree whereas Fleckeles was addressing a situation arising out of conflict with the civil law, which since Landau's time had been reaffirmed.

The Landau-Fleckeles approach in the struggle to maintain the primacy of Jewish law in the conflict-of-laws situations stemming from the state's interest in marriage regulation was not the only response to the challenge. In 1804, Rabbi Abraham Eliezer ha-Levi of Trieste put forward a sweeping proposal for averting the problems posed by the *Ehepatent*. He suggested that each community enact a *takkanah* requiring that all marriages be effectuated in compliance with the terms of state law.[72] Violation of the *takkanah* would result in excommunication of the parties and the nullification of the *kiddushin*.[73] This concept was not without precedent.[74] In the thirteenth century, the Rosh, in response to a question about the legality of a *takkanah* nullifying *kiddushin* without parental consent, held that such a *takkanah* was effective, under the principle that *kiddushin* was subject to the consent of the sages.[75] Similarly, Rashba, in a case involving a communal ordinance that marriages be performed before a quorum of ten or be considered null and void, held that the community did not exceed its authority in issuing such a regulation, and that it was enforceable as promulgated.[76]

This view, however, was not the unanimous opinion of the medieval authorities.[77] Rabbi Simeon ben Zemaḥ Duran (1361–1444), for example, ruled that although the power of annulment was "on the books," because of the seriousness of the marriage relationship, latter-day courts were not empowered to act as their Talmudic predecessors to nullify *kiddushin*; the community ordinance might, however, require a *get*.[78] This was the position of Moses Isserles, who in his gloss to the *Shulkhan Arukh* codified: "A community which agreed and enacted that one who doesn't perform *kiddushin* before a quorum of ten, or some similar matter; [if] someone transgressed and effectuated *kiddushin*, we worry lest there be a valid *kiddushin* and require a *get*; even though the community specifically ordained that the *kiddushin* would be no *kiddushin* and that the money [involved in the *kiddushin*] would be *hefker*, nonetheless, we must be stringent in practice."[79]

The approach of Rabbi Abraham Eliezer ha-Levi would have internalized state requirements, thus eliminating the conflict-of-laws problem presented by the *Ehepatent*. In this regard, the proposal differed somewhat from previous *takkanot*. None of the earlier community ordinances had involved communal enactment of a state law. This fact, however, presented no legal difficulty.

Although the proposal received the approbation of some Sephardic rabbis,[80] it was rejected by the Ashkenazic authority, Rabbi Moses Sofer (1762–1839), whose approval its author sought. Sofer wrote two responsa denying the possibility of enacting such a *takkanah*, taking the view that present-day Jewish courts were not empowered to annul marriages. These responsa were written at a time when Trieste had been conquered by Napoleon, and there was apparently some hope that the *Ehepatent* would soon be abolished.[81]

This was the scope of rabbinic discussion on the appropriate response to the state's regulation of marriage in the generation before Napoleon. *Dina de-malkhuta dina* was not suggested as a solution to the problem. All authorities acknowledged that marriage was a matter involving *issur* (religious prohibition) and thus beyond the purview of the principle *dina de-malkhuta dina.*

The question of the effect of a state-required divorce decree on the finality of a *get* was put to Rabbi Akiva Eger (1761–1837) by the rabbinate of Berlin.[82] Prussian law required a state decree to terminate the last vestige of the marital bond. Without such a decree, the spouses, by state law, would inherit each other's property as though they were still married. Therefore, upon the execution of a *get*, the rabbis of Berlin adopted the practice of informing the parties that, notwithstanding the issuance of the *get*, their status in matters of inheritance under state law remained unchanged, pending a civil decree. Rabbi Akiva Eger, who was asked to respond to the validity of such a *get*, replied that a *get* issued pursuant to this practice would not be ineffective for failure to sever the relationship between the parties.[83] The marital bond had been broken by the *get;* all that remained was a property relationship, imposed by state law. Akiva Eger cited substantial rabbinic authority holding that *dina de-malkhuta dina* was inapplicable to matters of inheritance. Similarly, in connection with the question of the validity of wills drawn up in non-Jewish courts, Moses Sofer declared: "Heaven forefend that in such a case we apply *dina de-malkhuta dina* against the law of the holy Torah, for, if [we were to do] so, we would (thereby) annul all the laws of the Torah."[84] Sofer's statement is a fitting summary of the traditional rabbinic stance on the primacy of Jewish law. Recognition of the authority of foreign law would be destructive of Judaism. Only in the limited context of commercial law, and only based upon the authority of Jewish law, would state law be incorporated into Jewish practice.

The forces of absolutism and enlightenment had, by the closing decades of the eighteenth century, found combined expression in the enlightened despotism of Joseph II. The implications of these trends for the continuity of Jewish autonomy were becoming apparent. Nonetheless, rabbinic leaders could still hope to preserve the absolute authority of Jewish law in matters of *issura* (ritual prohibition). Certainly, His Majesty did not wish to disturb the religious life of his subjects. As sovereignty passed from the king to the people, however, and the Jewish community was transformed into individual citizens of the Mosaic persuasion, a new historical challenge confronted Jews and Judaism, and the definition of *dina de-malkhuta dina* became an issue of critical importance.

3. The French Revolution

In France the abolition of corporate society was to lead to the phenomenon of the Jew as state citizen. This new standing vis-à-vis the state called for a redefinition of *dina de-malkhuta dina*. Although the Revolution liberated the Jews, Napoleon demanded a definitive pronouncement on the relationship between Jewish law and the law of the state. Eighteenth-century France had two distinct populations of Jews. The smaller but more prosperous Portuguese nation, totaling about thirty-five hundred people, was centered in Bordeaux and Saint Esprit, a suburb of Bayonne.[1] The population of the German nation, which was scattered through hundreds of communities in Alsace, Metz, and Lorraine, exceeded thirty thousand, the majority of which was in Alsace.[2]

The Sephardic Jews of the southwest were the descendants of Marranos who had settled in France during the sixteenth and seventeenth centuries. Letters patent issued by Louis XV in 1723 confirmed the erstwhile new Christians in earlier residence and trade privileges and for the first time officially recognized them as Jews.[3]

Having developed juridical norms as Marranos, the Sephardim never attempted to acquire the privilege of autonomous civil jurisdiction, even after returning openly to Judaism. Moreover, in matters of religious ritual, lay leadership held sway over rabbinic authority. Thus, for example, the rabbi was forbidden to impose any penalties, publish any decisions, or marry any couple without the permission of the nation's syndic.[4] As for the piety of the lay leaders, the Palestinian traveler Rabbi Ḥaim Joseph David Azulai, writing in 1777–78, reported that he had observed serious violations of religious ritual among Bordeaux's leading families, as well as philosophical speculations tending to heresy.[5] Azulai found, further, that only the Pentateuch, not the oral law, was being taught in the Bordeaux Talmud Torah,[6] a development paralleling the educational reforms of the Berlin *maskilim*. By the latter half of the eighteenth century, the Portuguese nation largely identified with French language and culture and was committed to preserving the existing order.

In contrast to the Portuguese nation, the German nation was fragmented and impoverished. The Ashkenazic communities had come under French rule during various parts of the sixteenth, seventeenth, and eighteenth centuries. Each of the three major Ashkenazic communities was separately organized and enjoyed judicial autonomy.[7] The primary occupations to which the Jews of Alsace, Metz, and Lorraine were limited were moneylending, petty trading, and dealing in used clothing. There were, however, some wealthy Jews among the Ashkenazim who dealt in horses and cattle and as a consequence were of important service to the French military.[8] The Ashkenazic Jews were bound by stringent commercial and residence restrictions and faced strong anti-Jewish sentiment from the local population, feelings that were exacerbated by the creditor-debtor relationship that commonly existed between Jews and peasants.[9] At the time of the Revolution, the preponderance of Ashkenazic Jews in France was still Yiddish-speaking and alienated from French society.

The chasm that separated the Portuguese and German nations is reflected in the tract of the Sephardic Jew Isaac de Pinto, *Apologie pour la nation Juive*, published in 1762. The author maintained that it was essential to distinguish the Portuguese Jews from their co-religionists, for "they do not wear beards and are not different from other men in their clothing; the rich among them are devoted to learning, elegance and manners to the same degree as the other peoples in Europe, from whom they differ only in religion." The depressed masses of Ashkenazim were not as they were because of their religion but because of the relentless persecution to which they had been subjected. Improved conditions would result in a betterment of their way of life.[10]

Among intellectuals of the European Enlightenment, the issue of the improvement of the Jews was a topic of common discussion. One of the most significant works on the subject was Christian Wilhelm von Dohm's volume *Concerning the Amelioration of the Civil Status of the Jews*. Dohm undertook this work at the behest of Moses Mendelssohn, who had been asked by Cerf Berr, the leader of Alsatian Jewry, to prepare such a memorandum on behalf of the Jews of Alsace. Dohm's tract repeated Pinto's observation that oppression had corrupted the Jews' character; the Jewish religion was not inherently evil. Measures that would improve the educational and economic opportunities of the Jew would thus serve to improve his character. Dohm imagined that the separatist nature of Jewish law would erode once the Jews regarded society as their own: "[The] timid and petty spirit of ceremony which has sneaked into the present day Jewish religion is sure to disappear again as soon as wider horizons are opened to the Jews, as soon as they are accepted as members of the political society and can make its interests their own. They will then reform their religious laws and regulations according to the demands of society. They will go back to the freer and nobler ancient Mosaic Law, will explain and adapt it according to the changed times and conditions, and will find authorizations to do so alone in the Talmud."[11] Indeed, Dohm maintained, the Jews would be deeply attached to the country they inhabit because, unlike foreign settlers,[12] they had no other homeland.[13] Jews should continue to enjoy communal autonomy, including the power of excommunication, he asserted.[14] Juridical autonomy "will no more isolate them from the rest of the citizens of the state than a city or community living according to their own statutes."[15]

Negative reaction to Dohm's proposal was quickly forthcoming from Johann David Michaelis, professor of Oriental languages at the University of Göttingen. Michaelis argued that the law of Moses made citizenship and integration into the state impossible for the Jew:

> As long as the Jews continue to observe the Mosaic Laws, as long as they refuse, for example, to eat together with us and to form sincere friendship at the table, they will never become fully integrated in the way that Catholics, Lutherans, Germans, Wends, and French live together in one state. (I am not discussing isolated cases, but rather the Jews as a collective entity. . . .)
>
> One must mention something in addition to the law of

> Moses, which Herr Dohm seems not to have considered, and which casts doubt on the full and steadfast loyalty of the Jews to the state and the possibility of their full integration, namely their messianic expectation of a return to Palestine. The Jews will always see the state as a temporary home, which they will leave in the hour of their greatest happiness to return to Palestine.[16]

Thus the separatist rituals and messianic aspirations of the Jews rendered them unfit for citizenship. Even if it were argued that mercantilist concerns outweighed religious peculiarities, a case for the Jews could not be made: "For the power of the state does not depend on gold, alone, but rather, in large part, on the strength of its soldiers. And the Jews will not contribute soldiers to the state as long as they do not change their religious view."[17]

Not long after the appearance of a French translation of Dohm's book, which was published together with the *Toleranzpatent* of Joseph II in 1782, the French government appointed a special commission to prepare a new set of regulations for the governance of Alsatian Jewry. This commission presented its report in August 1783, and the following January Louis XVI abolished the special body tax that had been imposed on Alsatian Jews. Less welcome, however, was the issuance of new letters patent, July 10, 1784, which confirmed residence and occupational restrictions, required Jews without legal residence to leave Alsace within three months,[18] and established that henceforth Alsatian Jews were to ask the king's permission to marry. Although ostensibly there was some economic liberalization, all new rights were severely circumscribed. Thus, for example, although Jews were permitted to rent farms, they could not employ Christian laborers, nor could they reside in the locale of the farmland if it were not within the ordinary bounds of permitted domicile.[19]

The year following publication of these letters patent, the Royal Society of Arts and Sciences in Metz announced as a subject for an essay contest, "Are There Means of Making the Jews More Useful in France?" There were eventually nine contestants for the prize, which was to be awarded in 1787, three of whose essays were published. The published authors, the Abbé Henri Grégoire, the attorney Thiery, and the Polish Jew Zalkind Hourwitz, shared the view that a cessation of persecution and exposure to Western culture were prerequisites to the regeneration of the Jews.[20]

The essay of Grégoire is particularly noteworthy both because it was written by a man rooted in the teachings of the Catholic church and because of the prominent role the Abbé Grégoire was to play in the discussions of Jewish emancipation during the Revolution. Grégoire believed that the Jews formed a state within a state because they were never accepted as citizens of the countries they inhabited. Although there were religious practices, particularly Sabbath observance, that seemed to preclude the integration of Jews into such pursuits as agriculture, labor, and the military, "we have reason to believe that the Rabbis will relax upon that head, when their decisions come to be authorized by necessity, and the Jew will give up his scruples when he is warranted by the infallibility of his doctors." Not only was the Abbé Grégoire convinced that the Jews would adapt to the norms of French society, given the opportunity, he affirmed that religious liberty might well draw them toward conversion. In dealing with the Jewish question, however, an important distinction had to be made between Mosaic law and civil jurisprudence: "These are

59

separate things. Let us grant to the Jews complete liberty in the first article, and in everything that does not affect the property, liberty and honor of the citizen: in everything else let them be subject to the law of the nation. Let us leave, then, to the Rabbis, the right of passing sentence in affairs which merely concern religious rites, without having connection with government."[21] The political-religious distinction articulated by Moses Mendelssohn thus found expression in the essay of the churchman Grégoire.

In 1788, Chrétien Guillaume de Lamoignon de Malesherbes, who had headed the king's commission that fashioned the edict granting French Protestants civil rights,[22] was appointed by Louis XVI to undertake a similar task with regard to the Jews. The Sephardim of Bordeaux dispatched Solomon Lopes Dubec and Abraham Furtado to Paris to confer with Malesherbes. Cerf Berr was already in Paris lobbying for the removal of economic restrictions placed upon the Ashkenazim. Although the Revolution intervened before the Malesherbes commission could reach any conclusions, it is interesting in light of subsequent events that the Sephardic position was based on preserving the existing legal distinction between the Portuguese and German nations.[23] The Sephardim were concerned that were they to be considered equally with the Ashkenazim, the ensuing Jewish status might be less than that previously enjoyed by the Portuguese nation.

With the summoning of the Estates General, the difference between the status of the Portuguese and German nations was again much in evidence. Although the Sephardim participated in the general elections for the Estates General, the Jews of Alsace, Metz, and Lorraine were excluded. The Ashkenazim were, however, allowed to submit a report pressing their demands.[24] They sought fiscal equality, freedom of residence and vocation, and the retention of their communal structure and authority.[25] Unlike the Ashkenazim, the Sephardim had nothing to gain from calling special attention to their situation. Subsequent to the formation of the National Assembly, the Sephardim petitioned the Abbé Grégoire not to make a plea for the emancipation of the Jews.[26] The Jews of Paris, however, in an address to the assembly, August 26, 1789, asked for full equality of citizenship and explicitly renounced corporate Jewish existence.[27]

The issue of Jewish emancipation was voted upon on December 24 on a motion that all citizens, including Jews, be admitted to public office. The motion failed. The arguments that prevailed were twofold: first, the Jews were a "nation within a nation" and could not be assimilated; second, granting the Jews citizenship would result in the destruction of Alsatian Jewry by the Christian population.[28] These two arguments were to be of major significance in the decade ahead.

The view of the Jew as a nation within a nation gained widespread currency during the 1780s.[29] Ironically, the slogan was first used in connection with the Jews by François Hell, who was a central figure in the inflammation of circumstances underlying the second argument adduced against Jewish emancipation, namely, the repercussions such an act would have in Alsace. Alsatian peasants, long burdened by wars, taxes, duty services, payments of *rentes*, and the struggle for subsistence, had for decades contracted loans from Jewish creditors, whose commercial activity was largely restricted to this pursuit. During 1777–78, Alsace was inundated by masses of counterfeit receipts "signed" in Hebrew characters. When Jewish creditors requested payment of debts, they were presented with such receipts. This scheme, it emerged, was orchestrated by François Joseph Antoine Hell, bailiff of Landser (upper Alsace) and later a deputy in the National Assembly. Efforts were made by the Sovereign Council, the king's judicial administration in Alsace, to resolve the matter, but it caused a substantial deterioration of the Jews' economic situation.[30] The case of the false receipts highlighted the enmity of the Alsatian peasant debtors toward their Jewish creditors. Thus one ultrarevolutionist deputy could, in good conscience, argue against Jewish emancipation in the assembly debate, asserting that a decree granting the Jews of Alsace complete citizenship would also be their death sentence.[31]

By the negative decision of the National Assembly, the Jews of Bordeaux, who were active in municipal politics, found themselves deprived of a right they had assumed. They immediately launched a lobbying effort to gain recognition as active citizens. On January 28, 1790, the assembly decreed: "All the Jews known in France as Portuguese, Spanish, and Avignonese will continue to enjoy those rights which they have enjoyed until now and which are sanctioned in their favor by the letters patent; consequently, they will enjoy the rights of active citizens, when they fulfill the conditions required by the decrees of the assembly." Corporate privileges having been abolished by the National Assembly, the Portuguese nation disbanded its communal organization as the quid pro quo for active citizen status. But the Bordeaux Jews promptly established an Association de Bienfaisance to continue various communal functions.[32]

The assembly postponed the question of equality for

the Ashkenazim indefinitely. Finally, however, compelled by the principles of the Revolution to resolve this anomaly, the assembly, shortly before disbanding, admitted German Jews to the oath of citizenship:

> The National Assembly, considering that the conditions necessary to be a French citizen and to become an active citizen are determined by the Constitution, and that every man who meets the said conditions, takes the civic oath, and undertakes to fill all the duties which the Constitution imposes has a right to all the advantages it confers, cancels all adjournments, reservations and exceptions inserted in the most important decrees concerning individuals of the Jewish persuasion who shall take the civil oath, which oath will be regarded as a renunciation of all privileges and exceptions previously granted in their favor.[33]

By this decree, the Jews of northern France, who, but seven years earlier, had received a new corporate charter, were declared equal citizens of the French nation. Not only were corporate disabilities erased but corporate privileges, the most cherished of which was juridical autonomy, were eliminated. In many of the states of western Europe, the corporate status of the Jewish community was to be eradicated within two decades. Even Dohm, the champion of Jewish civic rights in the decade before the French Revolution, had not advocated, let alone anticipated, such far-reaching change. The efforts of seventeenth- and eighteenth-century monarchs to subordinate all subjects equally before the king had, with the French Revolution, culminated in full equality before the law. The law, however, was that of the "people," embodied in the Constitution. The range of issues which was to confront Jewish law remained to be seen.

Some of the Jews of Alsace-Lorraine greeted the status of citizen with great enthusiasm. Thus on the day the National Assembly extended active citizenship rights to all French Jewry, Berr Isaac Berr dispatched a "letter to his brethren" in Lorraine, extolling the French, whom God had chosen as the instruments for regenerating the Jews. The Jews, in response, must "divest ourselves entirely of that narrow spirit, of Corporation and Congregation, in all civil and political matters, not immediately connected with our spiritual laws, in these things we must absolutely appear simply as individuals, as Frenchmen."[34]

During the decade 1789–99, the Jews of France, along with other French citizens, suffered through periods of chaos, privation, and terror. The two men who were to figure most prominently in the proceedings of the Assembly of Notables and the ensuing Paris Sanhedrin (1806–7), Rabbi Joseph David Sinzheim and Abraham Furtado, both personally experienced the impact of the Terror.[35] Sinzheim wrote of this era:

It was in the year 1794, when the days of remembrance, the days of anger, arrived. The Lord opened his treasure and produced the instruments of His anger, and we said: we have been condemned. Were it not for the Lord's mercy on us, we would nearly all of us have disappeared and been lost, as they had proclaimed that they would destroy all the books written in Hebrew. Our numerous faults caused some scrolls of the Law and precious books to be burnt, and precious treasures were then pilfered. I had to hide away my books. In this period of trouble and anger, those who know the ways of the Talmud stopped travelling and the ways of Zion were desolate. The doors of the Temple were closed to study and to prayer. I could not even study one chapter of a well-known Mishnah. I was in exile and moved from city to city, from border to border. Finally, the Lord took pity on mankind, and freed the land from the evil beast. The anger disappeared and everyone returned to his home in peace.[36]

Sinzheim's account is steeped in classical Jewish texts, themes, and language. It reflects both his own rootedness in traditional Jewish learning and the familiarity of his audience, the Jews of Alsace-Lorraine and of the Ashkenazic *yeshivot*, with biblical and Talmudic literature. Furtado, who had been a member of the Girondist Popular Commission of Public Safety in Bordeaux, had to flee for his life because of political reasons during the Terror.

As evidenced in Sinzheim's account, efforts were made to suppress Jewish religious observance during the Terror. Thus, for example, the Jacobin club of Saint Esprit-les-Bayonne endeavored to confiscate all Sabbath candelabra, end the wearing of festive garments by Jews on the Jewish Sabbath, and coerce Jewish merchants to do business on the Sabbath. In Paris during the Terror, High Holiday services were held secretly in a cellar, while several Jews sang revolutionary songs in the courtyard to divert the attention of passers-by.[37] As was the case with church property generally, many synagogues and other Jewish properties were closed and nationalized during the Terror.[38]

Added to the political and religious difficulties faced by the Jews of France, many of which were common to all Frenchmen, was the unresolved matter of Jewish debts owing at the time of the Revolution. Several Jewish communities owed debts on loans contracted, frequently from Christian creditors, to meet communal obligations.[39] In October 1790, the National Assembly dissolved corporations, including religious commu nities, although Ashkenazic Jewry remained incorporated until September 28, 1791. The debts of these corporations were assumed by the government by successive decrees of June 14 and July 30, 1791, and by the law of August 15, 1793, none of which made special reference to the Jews. The syndics of the Jewish community had often underwritten the loans obtained from Christian creditors, and they were most anxious for a government decision nationalizing Jewish communal debts. On December 6, 1797, however, the Council of Five Hundred decided that the Jewish communities were not included in the earlier decrees nationalizing corporate debts. The result was the continued existence of a Jewish community structure, operating under the title "Commissions in Charge of Liquidation of the Debts," empowered to levy taxes and prosecute tax delinquents and exercising control over all communal Jewish properties.

At the same time that the organized Jewish community was being reduced by external forces to a collection agency, there were significant manifestations of an internal erosion of religious loyalties. Thus, for example, the battle against Jewish religious observance in Saint Esprit-les-Bayonne was spearheaded by Jewish Jacobins. A new phenomenon, mixed marriages, became a symbol of the revolutionary era. With the introduction of civil marriage by the revolutionary government, a Jew no longer had to convert in order to marry a Christian.[40] Such marriages were regarded by revolutionaries, Jews and Christians alike, as evidence of the new spirit of equality and brotherhood. It is not surprising to read the demand of a Jacobin in Lorraine that Jewish men marry Christian women so that Jews and Christians would form one united family.[41]

For the Jews who struggled to maintain religious observance during the Revolution, the obligation of military service, which devolved upon them as citizens, posed a special problem. Indeed, the Jews in many communities sought exemption from duty in the National Guard on the Sabbath, generally without success.[42] As France sent its armies to other parts of Europe to spread the Revolution, this problem became common among European Jewry.[43]

In 1797, the Jews of Mantua, a part of the newly established Cisalpine Republic, sent an inquiry to Rabbi Ishmael of Modena, asking whether performing guard duty on the Sabbath was permissible. In his response, Rabbi Ishmael noted that he had sent a letter to the military authorities suggesting that the requirement of Sabbath service ran counter to the constitutional guarantee of the free exercise of religion.[44] Why, he wondered, could the Jews not exchange Sabbath duty for service on an alternate day? Ishmael recorded that he received a reply acknowledging the validity of his argument but asserting that the local populace demanded that the Jews serve on their Sabbath just as the Christians serve on theirs. Since the city had an eruv,[45] the authorities were not bent on subverting Jewish observance, and the situation that might result from the refusal of Jews to serve was fraught with danger, Rabbi Ishmael concluded that the required guard duty could be performed on the Sabbath. He added the prayer that "God may look from the heavens and send his help."[46]

In the early decades of the nineteenth century, Moses Sofer, the undisputed leader of Orthodox Jewry,[47] wrote a responsum in which he affirmed unequivocally the obligation of Jews conscripted for military duty in an equitable draft to carry out the required service.[48] The responsum declared that the draft law did not exceed the authority of the kingdom, and it was within the taxation authority contemplated by the principle *dina demalkhuta dina*. If the law permitted a draftee to buy his way out of service or to send another individual in his stead—not uncommon provisions at the time—taking advantage of such exemptions was permitted; indeed, fellow Jews should assist their brethren in attempting to effect such arrangements. But, continued Sofer, to coerce persons to serve, even if they were licentious or Sabbath desecrators, so as to relieve one who had been drafted from performing his military obligation, violated the biblical injunction against kidnapping and selling a man.[49]

These responsa reflect the concerns that had traditionally characterized rabbinic discussion of the *halakha* on military service.[50] Rabbinic authorities affirmed the right of the king or the state to call men to arms in defense of the community and recognized the legitimacy of the draft, as long as it was fairly administered. Although traditionalists feared the adverse impact of military service on religious observance and lobbied for repeal of the draft as it applied to the Jews, Jewish religious reformers welcomed the draft as a major step toward gaining political equality.

From the same Italian campaign that gave rise to the inquiries of the Jewish community of Mantua there first appears a record of an encounter between the French General Napoleon Bonaparte and a Jewish community. An anonymous Hebrew chronicle, probably written shortly after the events it describes, records the deliverance of the Jews of Ancona by the French army, under the command of the "Redeemer of Italy," Bonaparte. The author notes that the Jews had translated his name to

Hebrew as *chelek tov,* "a good portion," for Bonaparte had delivered them. The Jews of Ancona, threatened by destruction at the hands of the local anti-Jewish populace, were blessed with salvation and joy such as would not be experienced until the coming of the Messiah, wrote the chronicler.[51] The Ancona chronicle reflects the gratitude of Italian Jewry to the French and to Napoleon, in particular, for their liberation from oppression.

Napoleon's second encounter with a Jewish community was in 1798–99, when he proceeded to the Middle East in the initial phase of his ill-fated scheme to conquer India from the British. In Cairo, he appointed two "High Priests of the Jewish Nation," who, together with seven counselors, were to regulate the affairs of the Jewish community.[52] The popular image of Napoleon as liberator and restorer of Israel's ancient glory was to linger long after his actions established otherwise.

The first decade of the revolutionary era saw little change in the Jews' occupational pursuits. Notwithstanding the elimination of legal restrictions, public opinion was still opposed to the Jews' owning land, and Christian masters were reluctant to take on Jewish apprentices.[53] Thus by the beginning of the nineteenth century, Alsatian authorities were complaining of Jewish usury more than ever before.[54]

The events of the closing decades of the eighteenth century had raised a series of questions about Jewish life in western Europe which awaited resolution. Which law, religious or state, was paramount in the sphere of family law? Were there religious obstacles to the full participation of Jews in civic life? Were there religious tenets that stood in the way of the Jews' social integration. Phrased differently, were the Jews first and foremost Jews, or were they citizens who professed the Jewish religion? The responsum of Rabbi Ishmael of Modena on Sabbath guard duty reflects not only the dilemma faced by observant Jews in the new political reality but also the expectation of non-Jews that, in the new age, Jews would accommodate themselves to the demands of citizenship. Proponents of the civic betterment of the Jews had anticipated that, given political rights and responsibilities, the Jews would change their ways. Clearly, the times called for renewed discussion of *dina de-malkhuta dina*. Napoleon was to bring the matter to a head.

4. The Napoleonic Phase

After a decade of revolution and instability, a weary France in 1799 elected General Napoleon Bonaparte first consul for ten years under a new constitution. Public opinion, desiring only the restoration of order, was prepared to concede virtually unlimited power to Napoleon, whose reputation had been made by the Italian and Egyptian campaigns. The first consul immediately set about the task of regulating the administration of government and bringing some uniformity to a chaotic legal system. Napoleon's reforms were embodied in the Civil Code, which was enacted section by section and finally completed in 1804.[1] Popular satisfaction with his accomplishments at home and abroad was reflected in his election as consul for life in 1802 and as emperor in 1804.

In dealing with the institutions of religion in French society, Napoleon sought, above all, a means of subordinating them to the state. Long before his rise to prominence, Napoleon had written:

The Napoleonic Phase

> It is axiomatic that Christianity, even the reformed kind, destroys the unity of the State: (1) because it is capable of weakening as well as of inspiring the trust which the people owe the representatives of the law; (2) because, such as it is constituted, Christianity contains a separate body which not only claims a share of the citizens' loyalty but is able even to counteract the aims of the government. And, besides, is it not true that that body (the clergy) is independent of the State? Surely this is so, since it is not subject to the same rules. Is it known for defending the fatherland, law, and freedom? No. Its kingdom is not of this world. Consequently, it is never civic-minded.[2]

During his second campaign in Italy in 1800, Napoleon began negotiations with Pope Pius VII toward a concordat between the Catholic church and the French state. His position was ostensibly rooted in Gallicanism, which maintained that the church in France had ecclesiastical liberties independent of papal jurisdiction. Unlike earlier expressions of Gallicanism, however, Napoleon's version permitted state involvement in church affairs. Notwithstanding the compromising nature of the first consul's demands, the pope was anxious to reach an accord that would rescue the church in France from the precarious position it had occupied during the more radical phase of the Revolution and from which it had not recovered. The agreement that emerged provided that Catholic clergy would henceforth be nominated by the first consul and only then be consecrated by the pope. Salaries of the Catholic clergy would be paid by the state. Bishops could control churches necessary for worship, and the church would be permitted to receive bequests and endowments. It was agreed, however, that the holders of former church properties nationalized during the Revolution would not be disturbed in their possession. The pope further agreed that the French government could issue such police regulations for religion as it deemed necessary. Pursuant to this last provision, Napoleon enacted Organic Articles for the Catholic Religion at the same time he published the concordat with the pope, in 1802.

The Organic Articles provided that Catholic seminaries were to employ exlusively French teachers and to profess the principles of Gallican liberties. No papal bull was to enter the country without government approval. In addition, there would be one catechism for all France. This uniform catechism, which was adopted after Napoleon had become emperor, emphasized that the church was to be in the service of the state. It read in part:

Q. What are the duties of Christians with respect to the princes who govern them, and what are in particular our duties toward Napoleon I, our Emperor?

A. . . . love, respect, obedience, fidelity, military service, tributes ordered for the preservation and defense of the Empire and of his throne; we also owe him fervent prayers for his safety and for the spiritual and temporal prosperity of the State.

Q. Why do we have these duties towards our Emperor?

A. First, by bountifully bestowing talents on our Emperor both in peace and war, God has established him as our sovereign and has made him the minister of His power and His image on earth. To honor and serve our Emperor is therefore to honor and serve God himself. Secondly, because our Lord Jesus Christ . . . taught us what we owe to our sovereign . . . He has ordered us to give to Caesar what belongs to Caesar.

Q. Are there not special motives which must attach us more strongly to Napoleon, our Emperor?

A. Yes; for he is the one whom God has given us in difficult times to re-establish the public worship of the holy religion of our fathers and to be the protector of it. He has re-established and maintained public order by his profound and active wisdom; he defends the State with his powerful arm; he has become the Lord's annointed through the consecration which he received from the pontifical sovereign, head of the universal Church.

Q. What must one think of those who may fail in their duty toward our Emperor?

A. According to the apostle Paul, they would resist the established order of God himself and would be worthy of eternal damnation.[3]

Similar articles were drafted and implemented for the regulation of Protestants in France. The government named all Protestant seminary teachers, paid ministers' salaries, and assumed the right of approving all church doctrinal decisions. Only French nationals could serve as clergymen, and they were forbidden to have relations with any foreign authority.[4]

The Jews were considered not only a religious group to be regulated by the state but a "nation within a nation," necessitating the adoption of extraordinary measures. In January 1806, while returning from his German campaign, Napoleon stopped briefly in Strasbourg, where he gave audience to several deputations of farmers and landowners who brought claims against Jewish usury. Contemporary accounts agree that it was at this time that the emperor decided to act on the Jewish problem.[5] During the same month, the lawyer Poujoul wrote a tract on the Jews of Alsace, alleging that Alsatian Jewry had severely abused the freedom granted them by the Revolution. They had accumulated millions of livres of mortgages, did not attend public schools, shunned military service, and had failed to reform their odious religious code, he asserted. In sum, the Jews had not become useful citizens. Poujoul proposed a reduction in the value of the Jews' loans, the suspension of citizenship, and a reform of the Jewish religion, under government supervision.[6]

It is not known whether Napoleon read this work, but he soon expressed similar sentiments. In March 1806, he directed the legislative section of his Council of State to consider ways of dealing with the Jews. In a meeting with the council on April 30, 1806, he declared:

> The French government cannot stand by indifferently while a contemptible and degraded nation which is capable of the lowest deeds assumes exclusive ownership of the two beautiful departments of old Alsace. The Jews must be regarded as a nation, not as a sect. They are a nation within the nation. . . .
>
> It would be dangerous to let the keys of France—Strasbourg and Alsace—fall into the hands of a nation of spies who have no attachment to the fatherland. Formerly, the Jews were not even allowed to spend the night in Strasbourg. Perhaps it would be advisable to enact a law which would set the number of Jews permitted to reside in the departments of Haut-Rhin and Bas-Rhin at fifty thousand. The excess of that population could spread itself through the rest of France at will.
>
> One also might forbid them to practice commerce, on the ground that they dishonor it by taking usury, and void their past transactions as being tainted by fraud.[7]

From his remarks, it is clear that Napoleon's actions directed at the Jews were based upon his assessment of

Alsatian Jewry. Nonetheless, his measures in regard to the "Jewish problem" were not wholly limited to the Jews of Alsace. In an imperial decree published in May 1806, Napoleon accused the Jews in the northern departments of the empire of enormous usury and placed a moratorium on judgments rendered in favor of Jews against farmers in several departments. Further, he called for an assembly of the principal Jews to seek out ways "to replace the shameful expediency to which many among them have devoted themselves from father to son for many centuries."[8] A list appended to the decree specified the number of deputies from among the rabbis, landholders, and other distinguished Jews who were to be chosen by the prefects of these departments. In the other departments, the prefects were empowered to name one deputy for a Jewish population of one hundred to five hundred persons, two deputies for a Jewish population of five hundred to one thousand, and so on. The deputies so designated were to arrive in Paris by July 10 and await further instructions. Pursuant to this decree, 82 notables were selected, along with 13 supplementary deputies from Italian departments. A decree promulgated July 10, 1806, provided for the appointment of a delegation from the kingdom of Italy. Sixteen deputies were thus added, bringing the total number of deputies to the Assembly of Notables to 111, although all of them were seldom, if ever, present at the same time in Paris. In the year of Napoleon's decree, 1806, a pamphlet titled *The First Steps of the Jewish Nation toward Happiness under the Auspices of the Great Monarch Napoleon* appeared in Paris.[9] The author, Israel Jacobson (1768–1828), who as *Landrabbiner* and *Kammeragent* had struggled for the civic improvement of his fellow Jews in the Duchy of Brunswick for over a decade, proposed that Napoleon establish a Jewish supreme council, with its seat in France.[10] The supreme council, headed by a patriarch, would have the authority to enact such measures as would enable every Jew to perform his duties as a citizen. Within each district of Jewish population, synods charged with deciding religious matters and naming local rabbis would operate under the jurisdiction of the French government and the Jewish supreme council. As the political and spiritual bonds that enslaved Jewry were broken, declared Jacobson, the Jew would ascend to the level of his fellow citizens.[11]

On July 22, Napoleon appointed three commissioners to the Jewish assembly, Louis-Mathieu Molé, Etienne Denis Pasquier, and the younger Joseph Marie Portalis (son of the minister of cults). At the same time, he communicated the text of the questions to be put to the assembly, with the objective of "reconciling the belief of the Jews with the duties of Frenchmen, and to make them useful citizens."[12] The emperor posed twelve questions:

1. Is it lawful for Jews to marry several women?

2. Is divorce allowed by the Jewish religion? Is divorce valid, even when not pronounced by courts of justice and by virtue of laws that contradict the French code?

3. Can a Jewess marry a Christian, or a Christian woman a Jew? Or does the law order the Jews to marry only among themselves?

4. In the Jews' eyes, are Frenchmen considered as brethren or as strangers?

5. In either case, what relations does their law prescribe for them toward Frenchmen who are not of their religion?

6. Do the Jews born in France, and treated by the

laws as French citizens, acknowledge France as their country? Are they bound to defend it? Are they bound to obey its laws and to follow all the provisions of the Civil Code?

7. Who appoints the rabbis?

8. What police jurisdiction do rabbis exert among Jews? What judicial power do they exert among them?

9. Are these forms of election, this police jurisdiction, requested by their law or only sanctioned by custom?

10. Are there professions which are forbidden to Jews by their law?

11. Does the law of the Jews forbid them to take usury from their brethren?

12. Does it forbid them, or does it allow them, to take usury from strangers?

A clear symbol of the challenge of the state to the place of religion in the life of the Jews was the insistence that the assembly convene for its first session on Saturday, July 26. The deputies met for Sabbath services that morning and proceeded to the meeting, which had been called for eleven o'clock. Rabbi Lipmann of Colmar, the senior member of the assembly, presided over the initial meeting, during which Abraham Furtado of Bordeaux was elected chairman.[13] At the session of July 29, Messieurs Molé, Portalis, and Pasquier appeared on behalf of the emperor. Their desire, reported Molé, who served as senior representative of Napoleon to the Assembly of Notables, was to report to the emperor that the Jews were resolved to conform to the laws of France: "The wish of his majesty is, that you should be Frenchmen, it remains with you to accept of the proferred title, without forgetting that, to prove unworthy of it, would be renouncing it altogether."[14] The threat was clear: if the notables could not indicate that the Jews of the empire identified themselves above all else as Frenchmen, the Jews would be found unworthy of citizenship. Furtado, in his reply to the commissioners, expressed gratitude to the emperor, under whose protecting genius the habits occasioned by the Jews' long state of oppression would be reformed.[15] He appointed a committee of twelve, including three rabbis, to prepare the groundwork for the discussions of the assembly, which had received the text of the questions from the commissioners.

Upon reconvening on August 4, 1806, the assembly adopted a declaration, which was to precede its answers to the twelve questions. The declaration read:

> The assembly, impressed with a deep sense of gratitude, love, respect, and admiration for the sacred person of his Imperial Majesty, declares, in the name of all Frenchmen professing the religion of Moses, that they are fully determined to prove worthy of the favors His Majesty intends for them, by scrupulously conforming to his parental intentions; that their religion makes it their duty to consider the law of the prince as the supreme law in civil and political matters, that, consequently, should their religious code, or its various interpretations, contain civil or political commands, at variance with those of the French Code, those commands would, of course, cease to influence and govern them, since they must, above all, acknowledge and obey the laws of the prince.[16]

At first glance, the declaration seems to be a simple expression of the principle *dina de-malkhuta dina*. A careful reading, however, reveals that its scope is not limited to monetary matters *(mamona)*. The broad statement that the Jewish religious code is subordinate to the state's civil and political laws makes no distinction between monetary and ritual matters (*mamona-issura*).[17] Nonetheless, the basis of authority for the civil-religious distinction is clearly Jewish law. The terminology of the assembly's statement of principles has a familiar tone. Mendelssohn, one generation earlier, had distinguished between elements of the Mosaic constitution which were no longer applicable since the dissolution of the nation's civil bonds, and the religious laws which were strictly binding. Indeed, Mendelssohn quoted, approvingly, Jesus' counsel: "Render unto Caesar what is Caesar's, and unto God what is God's."[18] Although Mendelssohn's distinction did not run counter to traditional concepts of the authority and application of *dina de-malkhuta dina,* his language, which distinguished between religious and civil law, lent itself to a more expansive reading. Mendelssohn's name was invoked by deputies during the assembly's proceedings on several occasions.[19]

The assembly's preliminary declaration was, of course, only a dictum. The answers reflect the compromises which, of necessity, were made by the deputies, who included Ashkenazim and Sephardim, rich and poor, traditionalists and secularists. That the traditionalists figured prominently in the formulation of the responses is evidenced by the inclusion of proof texts adduced in support of the various answers, rather than a simple reaffirmation of the principle of submission to state law.[20] Notwithstanding the rhetoric of abdication, an effort was made to base the responses on specific *halakhic* grounds. Although the responses rested upon Jewish sources and precedent, in the main, biblical quotations, not rabbinic texts, were brought to bear on the matters at issue. There may be several reasons for this bias. First, the deputies were well aware of the prevailing view that the Jewish religion had become corrupted by accretions and rabbinic sophistry. Simple answers based on "Old Testament" texts would appeal more favorably to the emperor. Second, the nontraditionalists, who constituted a substantial segment of the assembly, tended to share this negative view of rabbinic literature and, in any case, were not as conversant with it as with the Bible. Finally, the traditionalists surely viewed these responses in a different light than "common" responsa, which were replies to observant Jews' inquiries about specific Jewish legal matters. This set of questions, calling for the definition of Judaism in postcorporate western European society, demanded a general set of guidelines. When observant Jews later encountered particular dilemmas, the rabbis would formulate more detailed replies.

Sinzheim, who, as a member of the "committee of twelve," played an important role in drafting the assembly's responses, corresponded with some of the greatest Jewish legal authorities in Europe during the period 1806–07. In a letter to Baruch Jeiteles, chief rabbi of Prague, he reported that he had successfully prevented any deviations from Jewish law in the answers of the assembly.[21] Close examination of the answers bears out, in the main, Sinzheim's claim of *halakhic* legitimacy.

In its reply to the first question, the assembly asserted that, though polygamy had, at one time, been practiced among the Jews, the *ḥerem de-Rabbenu Gershom*[22] had banned the practice and it no longer existed among European Jewry. Implicit in this response is the statement that a rabbinic synod is empowered to enact legal measures binding upon the Jewish people. This statement is double-edged: first, it calls into question the religious authority of a nonrabbinic assembly; second, it suggests the possibility of convening a duly authorized synod to enact new regulations. In any case, it is clearly grounded in internal Jewish legal principles.

The second response opened with a declaration that a Jewish divorce was valid only if previously pronounced by the French Civil Code. Although no Jewish law was violated by securing a prior civil decree, the absence of such a decree had never been held to impair the validity of a properly issued *get*. Indeed, an analogy may be drawn to the case of *kiddushin* enacted without state authorization, a circumstance under which, as Ezekiel Landau had affirmed, the validity of the *kiddushin* would not be impaired.[23] Consonant with the traditionalists' attempt to root the assembly's replies in Jewish law, this extension of *dina de-malkhuta dina* to an issue of family law required a *halakhic* rationale, and it is not surprising that the one reference in the responses to the *Shulkhan Arukh* appears in connection therewith:

> According to the Rabbis who have written on the civil code of the Jews, such as Joseph Caro in the Even ha-Ezer, repudiation is valid only in case there should be no opposition of any kind. And as the law of the state would form an opposition, in point of civil interests—since one of the parties could avail himself or herself of it against the other—it necessarily follows that, under the influence of the civil code, rabbinical repudiation cannot be valid. Consequently, since the time the Jews have begun to enter into engagements before the civil officer, no one, attached to religious practices, can repudiate his wife but by the law of the state, and that prescribed by the law of Moses.[24]

It will be recalled that the Bible requires a bill of "cutting off" to effectuate a divorce.[25] Based upon this requirement of a total severance of the marital relationship, the rabbis held that if, at the time of the issuance of the get, there remained an as yet unfulfilled condition, the get was ineffectual.[26] The assembly now declared that a failure to comply with state law would leave the marital tie unsevered because one of the parties could attack the get as incomplete. This *halakhic* support is novel in acknowledging that noncompliance with state law may provide a *halakhic* basis for challenging the validity of a get. Indeed, the assembly's response seemingly ran counter to contemporary responsa, which held that issuance of a get severed the marital bond, even absent a civil divorce.[27] In neither of the previously cited cases, however, had the state unequivocally declared the insufficiency of a get without a state decree. The assembly was thus dealing with a situation sui generis.

The assembly's recognition that there were Jews to whom religious law no longer mattered was manifested by the qualification that its answer spoke to those "attached to the religious practices." The terms of the response established concurrent jurisdiction between state and religion in marriage and divorce law.[28] As a final rationale for extending *dina de-malkhuta* to the field of family law, the response invoked the contractual theory of Samuel's principle: the rabbis, having sworn allegiance to the sovereign, agreed thereby to incorporate his demands into their juridical proceedings.

It is instructive to compare the assembly's response to this and other questions with the responses written by Rabbi Ishmael of Modena.[29] Rabbi Ishmael, who was eighty-three years old at the time the assembly convened, did not attend the proceedings in Paris. He did, however, formulate responses to Napoleon's questions, presumably as a guide to the Italian deputies.[30] In his answer to question 2, Rabbi Ishmael declared, "*dina-de-*

malkhuta dina," and further asserted that in all instances in which compliance with a law of the state did not violate Jewish law, its fulfillment was obligatory under this principle. This conclusion, which Rabbi Ishmael drew by specific reference to Samuel's dictum, the assembly preferred to reach by contract theory. Similarly, the argument of the "incomplete" divorce, absent a state decree, which the assembly based upon a general reference to the Even ha-Ezer, is found in the response of Rabbi Ishmael, based upon extensive citations to the Talmud, Maimonides, and the *Shulkhan Arukh*. Notwithstanding these differences in emphasis and style, the answer reflects the same line of reasoning and arrives at the identical conclusion as that of the Assembly of Notables.

The record of the assembly's meeting of August 4 indicates heated debate on the response to question 3, dealing with marriages between Jews and Christians. The answer, as adopted, distinguished between the seven Canaanite nations, with whom intermarriage was biblically proscribed, and the modern nations of the world, which were not considered idolatrous and with whom intermarriage was not explicitly forbidden.[31] The response noted that at various times and places there had been marriages between Jews and Christians. For obvious reasons, it did not mention that Jewish law, since Talmudic times, had viewed such liaisons as having no legal consequence.[32] For the present day, the assembly distinguished between religious marriage *(kiddushin)* and civil marriage. Although the former could be effectuated only between two Jews, the latter functioned by state regulation. A couple who married by state regulation "would then be considered married civilly, but not religiously."[33] Though Jewish law did not recognize such a legal institution as civil marriage, even the traditionalists of the assembly had little choice but to concede that such unions were taking place. The statement that the couple would be considered civilly wed was thus an acknowledgment of the existing reality, not the establishment of a new Jewish legal category. For those conversant with Jewish law, this point was emphasized by the statement that a couple married civilly could separate without a religious divorce. Since the civil union was "mere license," there was no need of a *get*. For those not sensitive to this *halakhic* nicety, the statement must have appeared as a further concession to the law of the state. The response observed that a Jew who married a Christian did not thereby cease to be considered a Jew.[34] Owing, no doubt, to the strong feelings of the rabbinic members of the assembly on the subject, the closing paragraph of the answer commented that the rabbis "would be no more inclined to bless the union of a Jewess with a Christian, or of a Jew with a Christian woman, than Catholic priests themselves would be disposed to sanction unions of this kind."[35] Rabbi Ishmael, who did not have to confront Napoleon or his commissioners personally, cited extensive rabbinic authority denying the possibility of *kiddushin* between a Jew and a non-Jew and did not address the status of civil marriage unions.[36]

The record of the discussions on question 4, regarding the brotherhood of Jews with fellow Frenchmen, reveals an attempt to insert a paragraph distinguishing between the Jews of the northern departments and those of the south. One might speculate that the Sephardic deputies wanted to remind the emperor and his officials that they had long been integrated into French society. As approved, the fourth response quoted a series of biblical verses which had exhorted the Jews to love strangers as brethren when they enjoyed national sovereignty. How much more applicable is this sentiment when the Jews live in a land that bestows upon them such favors and protection as does France, exclaimed the assembly. From among the more popular passages of rabbinic literature, the answer invoked the duties of Jews toward those who observe the Noaḥide laws and recorded the story of Hillel and his statement of the golden rule as the essence of Judaism. In sum, "Yes, France is our country; all Frenchmen are our brethren."[37] This said, the answer to the fifth question required no elaboration: the Jews no longer formed a nation, and they treated fellow Frenchmen in the same manner as fellow Jews.

The sixth question, concerning the obligations of military service and of conforming to the laws of the Civil Code, struck at core issues in the complaints about the Jews' alleged abuse of citizenship. The assembly's answer affirmed the Jews' duty to defend their country, based upon Jeremiah's exhortation to the Babylonian exiles to regard Babylon as their home. The response went on to declare that the Jews were so bound up with their country that a French Jew would feel himself a stranger in England, among Jewish company, and vice versa. Judaism was thus merely a religious confession; it created no national bond between its adherents. Rabbi Ishmael, who had, on an earlier occasion, addressed the issue of military service, reiterated the obligation to serve and then devoted his attention to the latter part of the question: "Samuel has said *dina de-malkhuta dina* and, therefore, the matter is simple. . . . But ritual matters are not included in this, for surely the king grants permission to all the inhabitants of his state to fulfill the practices of their law, each one according to their religion.[38] This passage is highly reminiscent of the language of Eliezer Fleckeles, who had determined, a decade before, that Joseph II could not have intended to declare *kiddushin* null and void, for certainly he wished to permit his subjects to live in accordance with their religious law. Rabbi Ishmael added, however, that this statement should be read together with his comment in answer 2, indicating that *dina de-malkhuta* demanded compliance with state law in all matters, to the extent that no violation of religious law was involved.

Questions 7, 8, and 9, dealing with the selection and authority of the rabbis, were answered in accord with the aforestated view of Judaism as a religious confession. The rabbis, asserted the assembly, exercise no manner of police jurisdiction. Whereas there was, at one time, a court system that governed the Jews, at the apex of which stood the Great Sanhedrin, latter-day rabbis were limited in their functions to "proclaiming morality in the temples, blessing marriages, and pronouncing divorces."[39] The answer of Rabbi Ishmael, whose years had spanned a long period of transition in Jewish life, is both poignant and revealing: "In days gone by, each community [of Jews] would attempt to receive privileges from the reigning ruler to permit them to act among themselves in accordance with the holy Torah and to place in ḥerem or to fine [violators], etc. Now, however, when everyone does what his heart desires and there is no power in the hand of the rabbis to protest, rabbis can only answer the ritual questions of those who inquire of them and preach to the people on matters of law and ethics and the love of their fellowman."[40] Corporate society had given way to individual citizenship, and regard for religious authority was now a matter of personal choice. Rabbi Ishmael acknowledged that the era of rabbinic jurisdiction over civil matters had come to a close as did, implicitly, the Paris Sanhedrin. At no point, however, did either party pronounce upon the permissibility of Jews resorting to non-Jewish judicial tribunals. Resort to *arkha'ot shel goyim* was an accepted reality. Such rabbinic courts as continued to function viewed themselves and were seen by the state as courts of arbitration.

On the question of Jewish religious restrictions that might prohibit the practice of certain professions, there was little to be said: "There are none," answered the assembly.[41] Questions 11 and 12, dealing with usury, were answered by resort to skillful biblical interpretation. At the outset, the response redefined the subject: lending money at interest, not usury, was the issue. Based upon the relevant passage in Deuteronomy, the assembly indicated that lending at interest to poor "brethren" (including non-Jewish fellow citizens) was forbidden, although commercial loans for profit were permitted.[42] Hence there was no Jewish legal distinction between the treatment of Jews and non-Jews in this regard.

In reviewing the responses of the assembly, one can see the basis of Sinzheim's remark to Jeiteles that the integrity of Jewish law had been maintained.[43] Although Judaism had been defined narrowly as a religious confession, no *halakha* had been violated.[44] The limits of *dina de-malkhuta dina* had not been narrowly drawn, but the assembly had insisted that Jewish law was the source of authority for the incorporation of state law into Jewish practice. In the matter of mixed marriage, the response of the notables implicitly denied their validity under Jewish law, conceding only the reality that such unions were legal by state regulation. Though the loss of communal autonomy was an accepted fact, the hope remained that the new age might be a glorious beginning. Sinzheim, in a speech delivered before the Assembly of Notables, declared:

> In the midst of these calamities [Jewish persecution in the Middle Ages] the Lord, about three centuries ago, took pity on our sufferings; he caused the dawn of philosophy to enlighten Europe, especially, some rays of hope gladdened our sight, and enlivened our prospects. Philosophy now diffuses its light over Europe; hearts are now opened everywhere to the mild sentiments of philanthropy and of tolerance. . . . If, till now we have seen only the dawn of happiness, this dawn will at last usher a pure and glorious light which will dissipate the last dark shades of ancient prejudices; all hearts will open to the noble enthusiasm of humanity, and we will see clearly the infinite wonder of the Supreme Creator as predicted by Daniel.[45]

In the meantime, it appeared that *dina de-malkhuta dina* could be successfully invoked to reconcile the demands of state law with those of *halakha* (Jewish law).

By the middle of August, the work of the notables seemed to have been completed. Sermons and odes to Napoleon filled the assembly's agenda. On September 18, 1806, Molé reported to the assembly that the emperor had, indeed, found its answers satisfactory. The Jews were to be secured in the free exercise of religious worship and in their political rights. In return, however, Napoleon required a religious pledge for the Jews' adherence to the principles set forth in the assembly's responses. As Molé expressed it: "Its answers, converted into decisions by another assembly, of a nature still more dignified and more religious, must find a place near the Talmud, and thus acquire, in the eyes of the Jews of all

89

countries and of all ages, the greatest possible authority."[46] A Grand Sanhedrin was to be established, charged with the task of converting the assembly's decisions into authoritative religious pronouncements. The assembly, which was to remain in existence until after the Sanhedrin had concluded its proceedings, was to select a committee of nine members to work with the commissioners in planning for the deliberations of the Sanhedrin as well as for the further discussions of the notables. The Sanhedrin was to have seventy members, exclusive of its president, two-thirds of whom were to be rabbis, including all of those rabbis of the assembly who had signed a letter of agreement with the assembly's decisions, and one-third lay members of the assembly, to be elected by ballot.

On September 24, the assembly adopted the text of a circular letter to be sent to the synagogues of the Western world, inviting them to send emissaries to the Grand Sanhedrin. Napoleon's objective in convening such a body, the letter proclaimed, "is to bring us back to the practice of our ancient virtues, and to preserve our holy religion in all its purity."[47] While awaiting the opening of the Sanhedrin's sessions, the assembly continued to meet.

In its sitting of December 9, the assembly heard a report from the committee of nine, describing a plan for the regulation of Jewish worship, which, it was related, had been devised in concert with the emperor's commissioners. The plan involved a division of France into a number of synagogues and consistories, which would be governed by a central consistory. The consistories were to assure that the rabbis' teachings were in compliance with the decisions of the Great Sanhedrin, to regulate and maintain synagogues, to encourage the

Jews' employment in useful professions and to report those without means, and to inform the government of the number of Jewish conscripts within each consistory.[48] The plan was, of course, accepted by the assembly.

The Paris Sanhedrin convened for the first time on February 4, 1807, and held a brief procedural meeting. The commissioners, who had become aware of the lack of respect with which the traditionalists of the north viewed the Jews of the south, arranged the appointment of David Sinzheim as *nasi*, president, of the Sanhedrin.[49] The format of the Sanhedrin's deliberations, which proceeded over eight sessions, from February 9 to March 9, was standard: the Sanhedrin heard reports delivered, primarily by Furtado, then unanimously adopted each decision.

As in the case of the assembly's responses, the doctrinal decisions of the Sanhedrin must be carefully scrutinized to determine their basis in Jewish law.[50] Again, the official statements were preceded by a preamble. This declaration, distinguishing between religious and political law in Judaism, was remarkably similar to the introduction suggested by Napoleon in his letter of November 29.[51] While paying lip service to its title as "Sanhedrin," the body claimed religious authority not on this basis but by the authority granted the sages of each generation to enact such ordinances as might be necessary for the preservation of the law. On this basis, proclaimed the Sanhedrin, any Jew of France or Italy who transgressed one of its enactments would bear his sin before the Lord.[52]

The first pronouncement of the Sanhedrin forbade polygamy, based upon the rationale set forth by the assembly: polygamy was contrary to state law and, furthermore, it had been outlawed by the Synod at Worms. Like the Synod at Worms, the Paris Sanhedrin did not declare that a polygamous union would be null and void; rather, it was "forbidden." The pronouncement added that a man whose wife was still alive could remarry only upon dissolution of the marriage by the Civil Code and by a proper *get* according to the law of Moses and Israel. Implicit in this formulation was the statement that a state divorce alone was insufficient to terminate *kiddushin*. The second pronouncement reiterated the notion that a marital relationship could no longer be fully severed, absent a state divorce decree before the issuance of a *get*. As in the first pronouncement, however, the Jewish legal consequence of a failure to comply with the Sanhedrin's ruling remained ambiguous. The Sanhedrin forbade any rabbi in the kingdoms of France and Italy to arrange a *get* unless the couple had first secured a civil decree. Any rabbi who transgressed this injunction would be considered "unfit to teach in Israel."[53] The possibility was left open, though, that a *get* so issued might be upheld. The third decision of the Sanhedrin did not deny the validity of *kiddushin*, absent a civil union. Rather, it forbade rabbis to arrange *kiddushin* without first assuring that a civil marriage had been effectuated.[54] The Sanhedrin repeated the assembly's assertion that mixed marriages were civilly binding, though of no religious standing, adding that Jewish partners of such unions would not be subject to ḥerem. Since the rabbis no longer had the power of ḥerem, this statement was gratuitous.

The fourth and fifth pronouncements ordained that the Jews of France and Italy regard and treat fellow Frenchmen as brethren. The sixth decision proceeded to the duties owed the state. The Sanhedrin decreed that it was incumbent upon the Jews of France and Italy "to view these nations as their homeland, to fight their wars and to obey, observe and carry out in their business dealings all that has been enacted in the book of the law of the state, called the Civil Code."[55] In carrying out their military service, Jews were exempt from commandments that might interfere with their duty. Interestingly, although the French text extends this exemption to the time of service (*pendant la durée de ce service*), the Hebrew text qualifies the exemption to a time of war (*kol zeman she-hem ḥayavim la'amod al mishmartam ve-la'avod avodatam ba-milḥamah*).[56]

The seventh decision urged Jews to implant in the youth of Israel the desire to practice all manner of noble professions, such as were encouraged by the Torah. It noted that the ire of the Jews' neighbors had sometimes been aroused by "certain practices" and directed Jews to do all they could to generate better feelings. In this spirit, decisions 8 and 9, dealing with moneylending, repeated the conclusions of the assembly, defining non-Jewish fellow citizens as "brethren," to whom loans were to be given free of interest when occasioned by impecunious circumstances and limited to the legally established rate of interest when given for commercial purposes.[57] Again, though in deference to the state the phrase *dina de-malkhuta dina* was broadly applied, the basis of its authority remained Jewish law.

At the conclusion of the Sanhedrin's work, it was only fitting that the *nasi* deliver a closing address. Sinzheim's speech provides excellent insight into the traditionalist view of what had been accomplished. The Sanhedrin, said Sinzheim, had recognized that there were religious and political laws in Judaism, but it had stood firm on the inviolability of the former: "You have recognized the

93

validity of certain civil acts, but you have acknowledged their religious incoherence. . . . You have recognized that certain usages were permitted in Palestine, but you have condemned them, here, as contrary to European practice. . . . In conformance with the precepts of the God of Israel, who is a God of peace, you have accepted that in certain public acts the civil sanction should precede the religious sanction."[58] The Sanhedrin, Sinzheim continued, had signed a "social pact" with Napoleon. The law of Israel is perfect and has no antisocial principles, emphasized the *nasi*. Hence the work of the Sanhedrin had not involved the slightest reform of Jewish law.[59]

Unbeknownst to the members of the assembly or the Sanhedrin, Napoleon had included in his instructions to his ministers a series of "regenerative" measures which he had in mind for the Jews.[60] Pursuant thereto, Minister of the Interior Champagny sent Molé a letter directing him to elicit from the assembly a statement soliciting the government to help resolve remaining problems.[61] Accordingly, Furtado, in good faith, drafted an arrêté inviting Napoleon to "take those actions which he believes to be appropriate, so that in the future some Israelites, either by second hand dealing, or, by taking mortgages, will be unable to cause the disorders in commerce and fortunes which have evoked complaints and which have too often brought shame and punishment upon all of their coreligionists."[62] This proposal, introduced March 25, 1807, elicited heated controversy in the assembly before finally gaining approval on March 30. With the ultimate adoption of this arrêté, the work of the assembly was at an end; the notables dispersed on April 6.[63]

Because Napoleon was in Poland, it was left to the

Council of State to devise a state program addressing the Jewish problem, which would carry out the emperor's mandate. On March 17, 1808, the emperor approved a series of three decrees regulating Jewish life in France. The first two decrees confirmed the consistorial plan of December 1806. The third decree established new restrictions on Jewish residence and business activity and imposed special requirements for Jews vis-à-vis military service.[64] The decree was to operate for ten years, in the hope that the Jewish condition would by then be "normalized"; if it were not, the decree would be extended.[65] The Jews of Bordeaux, Gironde, and Landes had not given cause for complaint and so were excluded from the terms of the third decree. Thus the work of the assembly and of the Sanhedrin had failed to ameliorate the civil status of the Jews. Its lasting legacy, apart from the establishment of Jewish consistories, was not in the emancipatory process per se but in the struggle to define the relations between Jewish law and the state in postcorporate European society. The guidelines so established, though never cited in a rabbinic responsum,[66] constitute the basis of Jewish accommodation in the Western world to the present day among those professing adherence to Jewish law. Just as Napoleon had forced the pope to come to terms with the new reality, so had he brought to a head the question of defining *dina de-malkhuta dina* for the new age.

The consistorial system adopted in France as the organizational structure of Jewish life was rapidly implemented in other parts of Europe under French influence. Thus, for example, Napoleon's brother, Jerome, appointed king of Westphalia in 1807, convened an Assembly of Jewish Notables in February 1808. Subsequent to its deliberations he established a Jewish consistory for the

kingdom, which included most of the land between
the Rhine and Elbe rivers. During the proceedings of the
Jewish notables, Jerome, who appears to have genuinely
favored equality for the Jews, gave audience to several
Jewish leaders. Not long afterward, he received a letter
from Napoleon, in which the emperor offered his unsolicited observations concerning the Jews. This letter,
written shortly before the March decrees, provides a
good look at Napoleon's thinking in regard to the Jews.

The letter, dated March 6, 1808, was critical of
Jerome's handling of various affairs of state, accusing
him of being guided by impetuousness and passion
rather than by reason. By far the greatest of Jerome's
follies, wrote the emperor, was the audience he had
given the Jews, "the most despicable of men."[67]
Napoleon's policy was to "correct" the Jews. By no
means, however, did he wish to take any action that
would increase their number within his states. Well after
the decisions of the assembly and Sanhedrin, the emperor continued to regard the Jews as a national problem; hence the Infamous Decrees.

The Westphalian consistory, which met in Cassel, the
kingdom's capital, was headed by Israel Jacobson, who
for more than a decade had labored to promote the educational aims of the *maskilim*. In addition to Jacobson,
the consistory included three moderately reformist rabbis, two Jewish lay leaders, and a Christian attorney,
who served as secretary. One of the lay members, David
Frankel, was editor of the German-Jewish periodical
Sulamith, the pages of which were filled with proposals
for the inner reform of Judaism.[68] Jacobson, who had
established a school at Seesen in 1801, founded a consistorial school in Cassel, as well as a seminary for the
training of teachers and rabbis. Religious services were

held at the consistorial school, over which Jacobson presided. These services were orderly affairs, at which chanting was prohibited and prayers and a sermon in the vernacular were instituted.

At Seesen, Jacobson financed the construction of a new temple attached to his school, in 1810. In a dedication ceremony brimming with Enlightenment era élan, Christian clergymen, the mayor and deputy mayor, the members of the Westphalian consistory, and other distinguished participants listened to a chorale presentation accompanied by seventy musicians, witnessed the removal of the Torah scrolls from the ark and their parade around the temple, and heard the reading of chapters of the Pentateuch in both Hebrew and German. The speakers at this celebration included the church counselor, Heineman, and, of course, Israel Jacobson, who was clad for the occasion in Protestant clerical garb. The enthusiasm of Jewish "progressives" at this event is reflected in the description of the festivities printed in *Sulamith*, which asked: "Where would one have seen a similar day on which Jews and Christians celebrated together in a common service in the presence of more than forty clergymen of both religions, and then sat down to eat and rejoice together in intimate company?" Jacobson's address is most revealing:

> It has been left to the tolerance of our days to bring about and to make possible that which only a little while ago would have appeared impossible. . . . If I do seek here first some rapprochement between you [fellow Israelites] and our Christian neighbours, I would ask more for your gratitude and honest help than for your criticism or even opposition. For your true and progressive enlightenment depends upon this rapprochement. On it depends the education of your spirit for true religiosity

97

and, at the same time also, your future greater political welfare.

Let us be honest, my brothers. Our ritual is still weighted down with religious customs which must be rightfully offensive to reason as well as to our Christian friends. . . . Our ecclesiastical office, the Israelite Consistory, is willing to help us.[69]

One can find in the speaker's remarks lingering elements of late eighteenth-century *haskalah* thought, as well as the program of early nineteenth-century reform. The Jewish religion, asserted Jacobson, was in a state of decay; there was much to be assimilated from the surrounding environment that would ennoble Judaism. Of at least equal significance in ritual reform was the dependence of the Jews' political status upon their religious improvement. Jewish practice must pass both the tests of reason and of suitability to the Christian world.[70] The state-established, Jacobson-led organ of Jewish leadership, the consistory, would lead the way in achieving the desideratum.

The consistory, which proceeded to enact various regulations for the ennoblement of Judaism, did not enjoy the support of religiously observant Jews. In an effort to demonstrate the Jewish legal basis for the consistory's rulings and, presumably, to gain support, Mendel Steinhardt (1768–1825), a rabbinic member of the consistory, issued a booklet of responsa in 1812, adducing proofs in support of ten specific matters on which the Westphalian consistory had published decisions. The preface to this work provides perspective on the ideological divisions in Jewish society of the time:

The masses of the people will not know or understand a word of this, for many are the simple Jews who, if presented with a matter as clear as the sun and as pure as the heavens, will seal their eyes from seeing and their ears from hearing, because for them, only the custom of their fathers is in their hands, and to every new matter which they have not yet heard they say "heaven forefend that we should rebel against God, the Lord of Israel, and commit a sin; thus have our fathers done in this city from ancient times, and we are, therefore, obliged to go in their footsteps and not to stray to the right or to the left." There are those who have the mind to understand and to hear in these teachings pleasing words, writings of uprightness and truth, but they refuse to draw from them, hardening their faces as stone, rather than acknowledging words which have not issued forth from themselves.[71]

The author's comments allude to three groups of Jews: the conservative masses, the better-educated but equally unyielding orthodox leaders, and the few, such as the author, enlightened individuals, who were both equipped and prepared to interpret Jewish law properly. Steinhardt made no reference to a growing fourth group, the element of Jewish society to which the observance of Jewish law was no longer of interest. Presumably such a work as his would have no appeal to these persons.[72]

The responsa began with the question of the permissibility of eating legumes during Passover. Within the normative Jewish legal tradition, the question is one admitting of alternative interpretations; indeed, to the present day, differences in practice exist between observant Ashkenazic Jews and Sephardic Jews. What makes the issue particularly noteworthy is the circumstance under which it arose: can a Jew serving in the military eat legumes during Passover?[73] The Westphalian consistory had, of course, to make some provision for the subsistence of Jewish soldiers during Passover. It could, however, have found narrow grounds for doing so, as had the Paris Sanhedrin.[74] It chose, rather, to issue a broader ruling, permitting the eating of legumes on Passover.[75] Steinhardt cited numerous rabbinic sources in support of the decision. This concern for the rabbinic precedent justifying ritual change was characteristic of early Jewish religious reform. Not until the following generation were more sweeping bases for ritual change postulated.

Most of the remaining responsa in Steinhardt's work dealt with reforms in the synagogue service. Among these were the introduction of a choir, the repertoire of which included songs in German, the elimination of *piyyutim* and of prayers asking for God's vengeance upon the Gentiles, and regulations promoting decorum in the service.[76] The Westphalian consistory also dispensed with *haliza*[77] for a widow whose brother-in-law was away at war and eliminated the recitation of *piyyutim* on the ninth of Av.[78] The latter deletion clearly reflected the feeling held by the *maskilim* that the European nations that had extended equality of citizenship to the Jews were, for their Jewish inhabitants, a new Jerusalem. No longer was there cause to bemoan the loss of a distant national past. Let it be understood among their Gentile brethren that the Israelites of the Mosaic persuasion were loyal citizens of the European state, with no other national aspirations.

With Napoleon's defeat at Leipzig in October 1813, the existence of Westphalia and its consistory drew toward a rapid close. In November, King Jerome left Cassel, and the following month Jacobson followed. The Westphalian consistory was at an end.[79] Many of its innovations, however, were to outlive its demise.[80]

In Italy, where the eighteenth century had brought no respite in the oppressive treatment of the Jews, Napoleon and the French were welcomed as liberators by the Jewish population.[81] Some of the legal issues confronting the Jews as citizens in Italy have been earlier noted, as has the participation of Italian Jewish deputies in the Assembly of Notables and Paris Sanhedrin. A further look at the new reality in which the Jews lived may be gleaned by examining the question put to David Sinzheim by Rabbi Yehiel Haim Viterbo (ca. 1776–ca. 1842) of Ancona in January 1810.[82]

Viterbo wrote that in a certain Italian city, it had long been the practice to hold a lottery on a particular Christian holiday, whereby a poor girl would receive a dowry. Many years after this event had become an established custom, "A king [Napoleon] reigned over all the cities and he was enlightened in his goodly righteousness to break the yoke of iron from the Children of Israel living under his rule, and he proclaimed: You [the Jews] are inhabitants as all the nations under my governance and there shall be one law for all." Accordingly, when the time came for the traditional lottery, the city's judges informed the Jews that they were to submit the names of seven poor Jewish girls to be included in the drawing. Viterbo had tentatively concluded that participation in the lottery was not *halakhically* justifiable. His conclusion was based upon Talmudic prohibitions against deriving benefit from idolaters during their holiday because so doing might be taken as an acknowledgment of the beliefs associated with the day or might arouse enmity. Moreover, it was not proper to accept charity from Gentiles and thereby to promote their merit. Not knowing what to do, he turned to Sinzheim, "for there is no guide as him among all the princes of Israel."[83]

Sinzheim found grounds upon which to base a ruling that participation in the lottery was permissible. First, the prohibition of deriving benefit from idolators on their holiday did not extend to Christians, who, for purposes of many Jewish legal matters, were not regarded as idolators. Second, there was, strictly speaking, no issue of enjoyment on a Gentile holiday in the present case, for although the lottery was held on the Christian holiday, the money was not awarded until later. As to accepting charity from Gentiles and thereby enhancing their merit, Sinzheim asserted: "In our day, when it is incumbent upon all of us to pray for the welfare of the king and his family as we do each year on every Sabbath and festival, this reason is not at all applicable . . . on the contrary, it is fitting that we act so as to heighten his merit."[84] As in his work in the assembly and Paris Sanhedrin, Sinzheim had skillfully effected an accommodation between the demands of the state and Jewish law.

When writing to the Italian rabbinate in his capacity as *ancien* (chairman) of the Central Consistory in Paris, Sinzheim was unable to effect such a masterful resolution. In the case reported, a Jewish woman, whose husband was in prison, had secured a civil divorce and was about to be remarried to a Jewish man in a civil ceremony.[85] Because a religious divorce had not been secured, the cohabitation of the woman with the second husband would, by Jewish law, be considered adultery.[86] Although with respect to *kiddushin* following a divorce, the rabbinate could demand that a *get*, in addition to the civil decree, have severed the first marital union, it was powerless to deal with individuals who bypassed Jewish law, as in the case at hand. The consistory, Sinzheim was obliged to respond, could deal only with religious affairs. He urged his rabbinic colleagues in Italy to use moral suasion to convince the parties to respect Jewish law. The limits of reconciling Jewish law with that of the state in the new era were starkly evidenced in this situation. Even in matters of family law, an area in which the Paris Sanhedrin had laid claim to concurrent jurisdiction,[87] Jewish law was ultimately subordinate to that of the state. This episode highlighted the inherent tension between religious and state law. Whereas traditionalist rabbis argued that Jewish law defined the limited areas in which state law was to be recognized under the principle *dina de-malkhuta dina,* the state regarded its own law as paramount, though it granted religious law a very limited measure of recognition in certain matters. In the generation ahead, some Jewish leaders would interpret *dina de-malkhuta dina* to mean that Jews were obliged by their religion to recognize the full range of laws promulgated by the state.

A consistory patterned on the French model was also established in the Netherlands, which, in 1795, was transformed into the Batavian Republic. The majority of Jews in Holland, who had long enjoyed relative freedom and prosperity, in addition to exercising the privilege of communal autonomy, were not receptive to the new order. Indeed, in the deliberations of the Batavian National Assembly, there were deputies who cited Jewish loyalty to the old regime as a reason to deny the Jews equal citizenship.[88] When as the price of citizenship, Jewish communal autonomy was abolished in September 1796, a liberal group of Ashkenazic Jews immediately established a new community under the name of Adat Jeshurun.[89] Among the reforms of the new group were the adoption of the Bible, rather than the Talmud, as the basis of Jewish education, the use of Dutch in the synagogue service, and the abolition of the practice of immediate burial of the dead.[90] The government-established Central Consistory, set up in 1808, was charged with the impossible task of governing all segments of Jewry, Sephardic and Ashkenazic, traditionalist and reformist. In reality, it functioned as little more than a government bureau for Jewish affairs. Upon the collapse of French government, Jewish sentiment against the continued existence of the consistory was so great that King William I provided the Jews of the Netherlands with a new organizational structure even before the constitution was approved.[91]

In Prussia, new currents of thought and a need for full national mobilization marked the first decade of the nineteenth century. David Friedlander's offer of quasi conversion to Christianity in return for civil equality aroused vigorous discussion.[92] In a tract published in Berlin in 1799, C. L. Paalzow urged the following "political" conditions as the quid pro quo for Jewish emancipation:

1. The Jews must no longer constitute a separate state within a state;
2. All ceremonial laws that prevent a Jew from carrying out his civil duties must be annulled;
3. The Jews must give up their own civil constitution;
4. The Jews must not meet in synagogues or private houses for the purpose of divine services;
5. All separate Jewish schools must be dissolved;
6. The Jews might use only the language of the country in all written transactions, books and accounts;
7. The Jews must permit mixed marriages;
8. They must serve in the army along with the other citizens.[93]

Among the many pamphlets that appeared in response to Friedlander's proposal was one written by the young theologian, Friederich Schleiermacher.[94] Schleiermacher maintained that such quasi conversions would be detrimental to Christianity because the opportunistic "converts" would inject elements of Judaism into Christianity. He suggested, instead, that the state grant civil equality to Jews who would renounce their belief in the Messiah and give up ceremonial laws that conflicted with the duties of citizenship.[95]

More ominous than the position that Judaism had to be reduced to a religious confession as the price of citizenship was the emerging spirit of German romanticism to which Johann Fichte gave expression in his *Speeches to the German Nation,* published in 1808. That the Jew was an alien who had no share in the history or destiny of the German *Volk* was obvious to the romantic. Indeed, early during the French Revolution Fichte had written:

> A powerful hostilely disposed nation is infiltrating almost every country in Europe. This nation is in a state of perpetual war with all these countries, severely afflicting their citizenry. I am referring to the Jewish nation. . . . It perceives all people as the descendants of those it drove out of its fervently loved fatherland. It condemned itself and is condemned to petty trade, which debilitates the body and deadens any tendency for noble feelings. The Jewish nation excluded itself from our meals, from our festive toasts, and from sweet, heart-to-heart exchanges of happiness with us by the most binding element of mankind—religion. It separates itself from all others in its duties and rights, from here until eternity.[96]

Notwithstanding such ideological trends, however, Frederick William III, under the influence of the liberal chancellor, Prince Hardenberg, responded to the calamity of 1806–07, the loss of more than half the territory of Prussia to Napoleon, by instituting a series of reforms designed to strengthen the power of the state. One such measure was the extension of citizenship to Prussia's Jews. The "Edict about the Civil Status of the Jews in Prussia," promulgated March 11, 1812, abolished all discriminatory taxes and occupational and residence restrictions, while imposing upon the Jews all duties of citizenship, including, of course, military service, the need of the hour. Jewish educational and religious affairs were to be regulated later, in consultation with Jewish leaders.[97]

So great was Jewish enthusiasm for the newly obtained status of state citizens that many did not wait to be drafted; hundred of Jews volunteered for military service. In Berlin, Eduard Kley and C. S. Gunsburg issued a call to arms in the following inspired words: "O what a heavenly feeling to possess a fatherland! O what a rapturous idea to be able to call a spot, a place, a nook one's own upon this lovely earth. . . . There upon the battlefield of honor where all hearts are animated by one spirit, where all work for a single goal; for their fatherland; there where he is best who submits most loyally to his King—there also will the barriers of prejudice come tumbling down. Hand in hand with your fellow soldiers you will complete the great work; they will not deny you the name of brother, for you have earned it."[98] If the Prussian state had emancipated the Jews, it remained for the Jews to demonstrate their readiness for full integration into the life of the fatherland. It is no wonder that Israel Jacobson headed to Berlin upon the fall of Westphalia—what better place could there be in which to carry on the work of religious reform?[99]

Although Jewish traditionalists actively resisted ritual reforms, the end of Jewish judicial authority and the almost complete resort of Jews to state courts were accepted with little reaction. In earlier times, *takkanot* had forbidden recourse to Gentile courts in no uncertain terms. With the erosion of traditional norms in the late seventeenth and early eighteenth centuries, resort to non-Jewish tribunals had become commonplace in western Europe,[100] a situation that was the subject of much invective by the rabbis.[101] Now, however, with the restructuring of church-state relations brought on by the modern state, there was no way to combat this practice. Indeed, *dina de-malkhuta dina* was invoked to authorize the heretofore illicit recourse to non-Jewish courts.[102] What remained of Jewish legal authority was an emasculated concurrent jurisdiction in matters of marriage and divorce[103] and Jewish law courts *(batei din)* operating as boards of arbitration, where permitted to do so by state law and when sought out by disputants. One can understand the comment of the Jewish traveler Jacob Sapir, who, in writing of the impact of Napoleon's legal reforms on western European Jewry, lamented: "In his [Napoleon's] days, the faces of Israel shone with physical freedom, but their eyes were dimmed by the subjugation of the soul, and the Torah donned sackcloth, for her glory was ended. . . . Napoleon gave the Jews liberty, freedom and equal rights of citizenship, without national distinction, but he took from them their standing in Torah and their religion . . . leaving to their Judaism naught but the worship of God . . . and there is no longer a court of law *(bet din)* which will assemble and judge the nation of God by the laws of the holy Torah."[104]

The defeat of Napoleon brought an end to the sweeping acts of emancipation that had characterized the generation of 1790 to 1815. Article XVI of the German Confederation, signed at the close of the Congress of Vienna, provided that

> the different Christian sects in the countries and territories of the German Confederation shall not experience any difference in the enjoyment of civil and political rights. The Diet shall consider of the means of effecting, in the most uniform manner, an amelioration in the civil state of those who profess the Jewish religion in Germany, and shall pay particular attention to the measures by which the enjoyment of civil rights shall be secured and guaranteed to them in the Confederated States, upon condition, however, of their submitting to all the obligations imposed upon other citizens. *In the meantime the privileges already granted to that sect by any particular state shall be secured to them.*[105]

The preposition "by" in connection with the grant of rights to the Jews "by any particular state" was inserted in place of "in," at the instigation of Bavaria, at the session at which the article was adopted on June 8, 1815. This changed rendering of the phrase was seized upon by conservatives as the legal basis for reversing the liberalization in the Jews' status accomplished by "alien" governments during the revolutionary era.[106]

In the reactionary period that ensued, Jews struggled to preserve the rights they had so recently won, responded in a variety of ways to the influence of romanticism, and wrestled with the continuing dilemma of the relationship between Jewish law and the state. As in the generation before, issues of religious thought and practice were often intertwined with political realities. In this milieu, the scope of the principle *dina de-malkhuta dina* was to be the subject of renewed controversy.

5. Religious Reform, 1815–1848

The political reaction that followed the defeat of Napoleon brought a return to the prerevolutionary era status of the Jews in the states of Italy and in all sections of the Austrian Empire. In the papal states Jews were restored to the ghetto, restricted in their movement, and obliged to listen to missionary sermons. Within the Austrian Empire, special taxes on Jews, limitations on the number of Jewish marriages, and regulations on Jewish domicile were again enforced. For the Jews of Austria-Hungary, who had never recognized the expansive application of *dina de-malkhuta dina*, the restoration of the old order was viewed as a blessing. The leader of Hungarian Jewry, Rabbi Moses Sofer, became the champion of conservatism in the emerging struggle against religious innovation. Not surprisingly, his treatment of *dina de-malkhuta* issues was confined to such questions as the king's right to alter the coinage system, the king's right to an inheritance tax, and the obligation to comply with the contractual forms stipulated by the kingdom.[1]

In France, the consistorial system survived Napoleon's defeat, and the relationship between the Jews and the state continued to exist within the framework of the doctrinal decisions of the Paris Sanhedrin. One consequence of the July 1830 French Revolution was the equalization of the Jews in the matter of state payment of the clergy. In the Netherlands, also, Jewish emancipation was preserved in the liberal constitution adopted upon the restoration of the House of Orange.

In Prussia and several of the smaller German states the struggle for full Jewish emancipation continued, and discussion of *dina de-malkhuta dina* was carried on with great vigor, extending even to non-Jewish circles.[2] Post-Napoleonic German nationalism was convinced of the centrality of Christianity to German national life. The implications of this notion for the emancipation of the Jews were clear. As one ideologist of German-Christian nationalism put it: "No man can serve two masters, and indeed it is only a strange contradiction that a citizen of the Jewish state or Kingdom should seek to be at the same time a citizen of a Christian state."[3] Even among those who did not insist upon conversion as a prerequisite for the Jews' citizenship, an emancipation from Jewish tradition was considered essential. The Jew must abandon the Talmud for "a wise morality of love of the homeland and universal love of mankind."[4] The price of emancipation was to be the assimilation of the Jew.

The growing sense that a "Jewish problem" existed owing to the alien identity of the Jew manifested itself in the legal status accorded German Jewry. Thus, although Prussia retained the most liberal legislation concerning the Jews in a German state until the revolutions of 1848, an amendment to the 1812 edict of emancipation, en-

111

acted in 1822, repealed the paragraph that authorized Jews to fill academic positions and hold municipal offices. This confusion between emancipation and assimilation was not unique to non-Jewish circles. The notion that Judaism must be reformed in order for the Jews to prove worthy of emancipation was shared by some Jewish intellectuals.

Nineteenth-century German-Jewish religious reformers attacked the Talmud in a line of criticism pursued by *maskilim* of the previous generation. As the Maskil Isaac Satanow had observed, commenting on the Talmudic saying "if our fathers were like men, we are like donkeys": "We are donkeys indeed to carry upon ourselves the many laws and statutes they loaded upon us through the Babylonian and Palestinian Talmuds."[5] This criticism was rooted in the work of Baruch Spinoza, who had maintained that Jewish ceremonials formed no part of the Divine law. Ultimately, this conception was a secularized version of the Christian insistence that the Jews were tied to rigid legalisms and had abandoned the spirit of the law.

Acting upon this view, Israel Jacobson had launched several efforts to establish reform in Jewish worship which would render the Jewish service more compatible with the German Christian environment.[6] Upon the closure of Jacobson's Berlin service, such reform activity spread to the Free City of Hamburg, under the leadership of Eduard Kley (1789–1867), who had preached at the Jacobson temple in Berlin. The New Israelitish Temple Association of Hamburg dedicated its temple in 1818 and used a newly prepared prayerbook, written largely in German, which deleted various prayers in an effort to abbreviate the service and omitted all national references, including the hope for the messianic redemption of Israel. An organ accompanied Sabbath services in the Hamburg temple. In support of these reforms, Eliezer Lieberman, commissioned by Israel Jacobson, secured and published a booklet of responsa obtained from two Hungarian and two Italian rabbis, approving of such changes.[7]

The Orthodox response to the innovations of the Hamburg Temple was published by the Beth Din of Hamburg, under the title *Eleh Divrei ha-Brit* (These are the words of the covenant). This work was a collection of letters from the leading traditionalist rabbis of Europe, concurring with the decisions of the Hamburg Beth Din in forbidding altering the traditional liturgy, worshiping in a language other than Hebrew, and using musical instruments in the synagogue on Sabbaths or festivals, even if such instruments were played by a non-Jew. It is clear from an examination of this text that the issue that aroused the greatest concern among the traditionalists was the matter of liturgical change, specifically, the implicit denial of the Jews' national and messianic aspirations: "Worse than all else was the deletion of all reference to the ingathering of the exiles. . . . This belief [in the messianic redemption of the Jews] does not at all oppose the honor of the kings and officers in whose shade we live, for they all know that we believe in the coming of the Messiah and the ingathering of exiles . . . but they also know that we are obligated to seek the peace of the nations which have brought us to the shade of their beam. . . . And whomsoever denies this belief DENIES AN ESSENTIAL PRINCIPLE OF FAITH."[8]

This theme was amplified by Moses Sofer in the first of three letters he submitted to the Hamburg rabbinical court: "We are now as captives of the war of the destruction [of the second Temple] and out of His abundant righteousness God has caused us to find grace in the eyes of the kings and officers of the nations . . . and they have never taken umbrage at this (our aspirations for messianic redemption) but perhaps *These Men* [the reformers] do not expect or do not believe in the words of our prophets . . . and all that has been related in this regard in the words of our sages of blessed memory." Similarly, Rabbi Mordecai Benet of Nikolsburg wrote: "One who says to omit the prayers for redemption because we live comfortably among the nations is utterly in error and is suspect of being an *apikoros*." The Beth Din of Prague, headed by Eliezer Fleckeles, was succinct in its remarks: "In truth, they are nonbelievers, and their intention is only to acquire a 'name' among the nations, so that they [the nations] will say that they are smarter than the rest of the Children of Israel; they are, in fact, neither Jews nor Christians."[9]

Obviously, the reformers did not view themselves as "captives of war" but, rather, as bona fide Germans. The traditionalists' lack of understanding of the reformist activity was reflected in the recurrent claim that the reformers were inconsistent, viewed from the framework of Jewish legal norms.[10] Notwithstanding such an exercise as the publication of *Nogah ha-Zedek*, the basis for the activity of the reformers was not Jewish law but the goals of integration into German society and complete political emancipation developed during the Enlightenment.[11] This radically different self-image was not understood by the opponents of reform and rendered the religious reforms of the nineteenth century different from those of previous centuries. For example, Renaissance-era rabbinic discussions had considered such issues as the permissibility of illuminating *ketubbot* and of choral singing in the synagogue service,[12] whereas emancipation-era deliberations extended to such matters as the legality of intermarriage and a fundamental reinterpretation of the Sabbath. The framework of these controversies was no longer specific Jewish legal norms. The principle *dina de-malkhuta dina*, however, underlay much of the debate over reform. The issue was progressively to become one of ultimate authority. Did the rabbis have the legal authority to define the limits of *dina de-malkhuta dina*, or did the state make this determination?

Frequently, appeal was made by the opposing parties to identical sources. In this regard, the contribution of a rabbi of Amsterdam to *Eleh Divrei ha-Brit* is of particular interest: "One who does not believe in the coming of the Messiah has no portion in the midst of the People of Israel and the name 'Israel' should no longer be applied to him . . . and according to these words have the eminent sages, our rabbis and teachers Moses Mendelssohn and Naphtali Herz Wessely written in our time."[13] The same Mendelssohn who was claimed by the early reformers as the forerunner of their activities was, not infrequently, invoked by the traditionalists to support their position. Similarly, the doctrinal decisions of the Paris Sanhedrin were to be cited by both traditionalists and reformers to sustain their conclusions concerning the relationship between Jewish law and the law of the state in the decades ahead.

Despite, or perhaps in reaction to, efforts at integration into German society on the part of Jewish reformers, anti-Jewish riots broke out in Wurzburg, Frankfurt, Heidelberg, Karlsruhe, Hamburg, and some thirty other cities in August and September 1819.[14] It was at this juncture that a new approach to the problem of controverting the negative image of the Jew emerged from within German Jewish intellectual circles, under the name *Wissenschaft des Judentums*. Two months after the riots, in November 1819, seven Jewish university students founded the Verein für Cultur und Wissenschaft der Juden in Berlin, with the avowed purpose of propagating the disciplined study of Judaism among their fellow Jews. One member of the society, Immanuel Wolf (Wohlwill), authored a document setting forth the basic principles of Jewish science:

1. The science of Judaism comprehends Judaism in its fullest scope;
2. It unfolds Judaism in accordance with its essence and describes it systematically, always relating individual features back to the fundamental principle of the whole;
3. It treats the object of study in and for itself, for its own sake, and not for any special purpose or definite intention. It begins without any preconceived opinion and is not concerned with the final result. Its aim is neither to put its object in a favorable, nor in an unfavorable light, in relation to prevailing views, but to show it as it is.[15]

Such scientific investigation, however, was not totally lacking in practical application: "Scientific knowledge of Judaism must decide on the merits or demerits of the Jews, their fitness or unfitness to be given the same status and respect as other citizens."[16] Although the Verein disbanded in 1823, one of its founding members, Leopold Zunz, was to devote the remainder of his long life to scientific Jewish scholarship.[17] In the preface to his first major work, *Die gottesdienstlichen Vortrage der Juden*, written in 1832,[18] Zunz clearly expressed the important practical aspect of Jewish science: "The civil disabilities of the Jews are bound up with the neglect of Jewish science. Through ampler spiritual culture and more profound knowledge of their own affairs, the Jews would not only have attained a higher degree of recognition and also of right, but could have avoided many a blunder of legislation and many a prejudice against Jewish antiquity, which are a direct consequence of the neglected condition in which, for the past seventy years, Jewish literature and the Science of Judaism find themselves in Germany."[19] Not only did *Wissenschaft* offer a means of scientifically establishing the merit of Judaism, it provided a rationale for the work of the generation-old movement for Jewish religious reform. Abraham Geiger, the leading ideologist of reform in its second generation, saw in *Wissenschaft* the means of ascertaining the objective basis for religious change: "The practical religious interest [in this endeavor] intends . . . to utilize the results gained from such investigations for the present time, and to perpetuate consciously *in accordance with the contemporary trend of development,* that which was created in olden times and transmitted to us, thus imbuing it with new life for the present time and its requirements."[20] In Geiger's view, Judaism had evolved through historical periods of revelation, tradition, and rigid legalism and was now at a time of liberation and criticism. Fundamental to the Jews' liberation was a renewed emphasis on universalism. For this reason, upon learning that Zunz was observing the Jewish dietary laws, Geiger wrote to him: "It is precisely these dietary laws that are so void of rationale and at the same time such a hindrance to the development of social relationships. Truly, the ideal of the deeper sense of brotherhood among men should have priority over the revival of that sense of separation which is both devoid of color and is of very

117

dubious value. Consequently, I could attach more value to almost anything rather than to this particular branch of rabbinic legal practice."[21] As manifest in Geiger's remarks, the goal of Jewish religious reform continued to be the Jews' integration into the larger society.

One area of rabbinic legal practice which Geiger proposed to revive was the exercise of the principle *Kol hamekadesh a-da'ata de rabbanan mekadesh*. In 1837, he published an article in his *Wissenschaftliche Zeitschrift* in which he suggested that this Talmudic principle be applied in such a way as to eliminate the need of a *get* upon termination of a marriage by civil decree.[22] If the state dissolved a marital union, let the rabbis declare the union void. Earlier in the century, a proposal had been made to invoke this authority to annul marriages entered into in contravention of the *Ehepatent* in Austria. This proposal, which aimed at accommodating to the state's prohibition of certain marriages, was rejected by the weight of traditional rabbinic authority because of a reluctance to exercise such sweeping power in the area of marriage and divorce law. Geiger's proposal was more radical than its predecessor in two respects. First, the earlier proposal was esentially a preventive measure. If Jews knew that their union would have no Jewish legal sanction, presumably they would not marry until complying with necessary regulations. Geiger's proposal was directed at the termination of marriages that might have been legitimate for many years prior to dissolution. Second, whereas the earlier proposal addressed a problem occasioned by a state law that actively declared the invalidity of various marital unions, Geiger spoke to a situation in which the state was not posing a difficulty with which Jewish law was obliged to grapple. There was no impediment to the issuance of a *get* in conjunction with civil divorce. Moreover, the Paris Sanhedrin had clearly affirmed the requirement that a *get*, together with the state decree, terminate a severed Jewish marital union.

Geiger's article did not create much of a sensation, in part perhaps because in the decades since the controversy over the Hamburg Temple prayerbook, the Orthodox rabbinate had concluded that the reformers were to be regarded as heretics, whose observations on Jewish law were not worthy of consideration. Until an immediate threat of reformist activity confronted them, they did not respond to reform proposals.[23] Furthermore, by the second generation of reform, most of the reformers' literature, including Geiger's proposal, was written in German, placing it outside the language competence of many traditionalist rabbis.

The romantic intellectual current then flourishing in Germany provided the background for the neo-Orthodoxy preached by Samson Raphael Hirsch (1808–88).[24] Hirsch set forth his approach to Judaism and its relationship to modern society in *The Nineteen Letters of Ben Uziel*, published in 1836.[25] In keeping with romantic thought, Hirsch maintained that the *Volksgeist*, in this case Judaism, could be understood only from within itself. Thus to comprehend Judaism properly, one had to accept the divinity of the Torah. The universe, wrote Hirsch, in a passage reflective of romantic natural philosophy, was one unified organism, interlinked in a continuous, reciprocal chain of love. Man's task, in this universal organism, was to fulfill the Divine will, as expressed in His Law. The law itself was an organism that had to be understood in its own mutual interdependence. Israel's mission was to promote the fulfillment of God's will through its total submission to

119

the Torah. Thus the national period in Israel's history was not an end in itself but only a means of carrying out this mission. The current age of mildness and justice offered an optimal opportunity for Israel to fulfill its mission. As for the Jews' relationship to the state, Israel's spiritual role by no means required its isolation from the state; to the contrary, "it is our duty to join ourselves as closely as possible to the state which receives us into its midst, to promote its welfare and not to consider our own well-being as in any way separate from that of the state to which we belong."[26] Thus despite strong ideological differences, religious reformers, students of Jewish science, and proponents of neo-Orthodoxy shared the common aspiration of Jewish political emancipation.

During the decade of the 1840s, Jewish religious reformers extended the application of *dina de-malkhuta dina* in two areas of law: Sabbath observance and marriage. In 1842, the reformist rabbi of Sachsen-Meiningen permitted and encouraged Jewish schoolchildren to write their lessons on the Sabbath, in accordance with Samuel's Talmudic dictum *dina de-malkhuta dina*.[27] If his duties as a citizen involved Sabbath violation, the rabbi asserted, a Jew was to ignore the Sabbath laws, for "the law of the kingdom is law." Here, the rupture of the traditional *issura-mamona* (religious prohibition-commercial) distinction is clearly evidenced. In effect, any demand of the state was to transcend Jewish law. In this version of the civil-religious distinction, the state determines what is in the category "civil" by the scope of its legislation.[28] Any matter which the state legislates is civil, and *dina de-malkhuta dina* applies. Such an approach had earlier been implied by Aaron Chorin, who had interpreted *dina de-malkhuta dina* to authorize the state to promulgate and enforce all manner of laws affecting Jewish life, as long as the intent of the enactments was to benefit the Jews and not to detract from their fulfillment of their religion.[29]

In the area of marriage and divorce, Samuel Holdheim, who advocated the application of *dina de-malkhuta dina* to this sphere of law, took a different approach.[30] He conceded the traditional *issuramamona* distinction but maintained that marriage law was properly a *mamona* matter. This conclusion followed from Holdheim's analysis of the processes of acquiring and separating from a wife.[31] Just as land, for example, could be acquired by money, deed, or evidence of presumptive ownership, so is a woman acquired by *kesef, shetar,* or *biah*.[32] As to divorce, just as a man can dispose of his property at will, so may he, biblically, divorce his wife at will. Having thus demonstrated that marriage and divorce were within the category *mamona*, Holdheim concluded that marriage and divorce were matters of state, not religious, jurisdiction. As a general matter, wrote Holdheim, all interhuman relationships should be governed by state law:

> That which is of an absolutely religious character and of a purely religious content in the Mosaic legislation and in the later historical development of Judaism—whether we call it divine tradition or human progress—and which refers to the relationship of man to God, his Heavenly Father, that has been commanded to the Jew by God for eternity. But whatever has reference to interhuman relationships of a political, legal, and civil character was originally meant to apply only to the given conditions of such a political and civil existence—as Scripture states innumerable times. Yet it must be totally deprived of its applicability, everywhere and forever, when Jews enter

121

into relationships with other states, or, at any rate, when they live outside the conditions of the state for which that law was originally given.[33]

Such a broad formulation transforms the *issura-mamona* distinction to the difference between commandments *bein adam la-makom* (between man and God) and *bein adam le-havero* (between man and man). Holdheim here suggests that only the former category is not subject to state legislation. In fact, Holdheim struggled with the problem of defining the respective parameters of the religious and the civil. Thus in a speech before the first Reform Rabbinical Conference in 1844, he declared: "It is difficult to keep the two separate, because they have been connected closely for so long a time. For this very reason it is important that two things which have been joined so improperly should be sundered finally. When and how shall this separation take place? That we cannot determine here and now, but it is the task of the present age. We do not grant that there is such a thing as a 'Christian state,' and certainly we should not speak of a 'Jewish state,' or of the overlapping of the religious and the political in Judaism. . . . Let the Jewish clergyman concern himself with religious instruction."[34] In a letter written to a small group of Jewish religious reformers in Hungary in 1848, Holdheim affirmed:

Now that the Jews have become integral elements of other peoples and states, in conjunction with whom they are determined to further the moral aims of society, all laws and institutions of Judaism which were based upon the election of a particular Jewish people—yes, of a particular Jewish state—and hence by their very nature implied exclusiveness and particularism, and served merely to strengthen the nationalistic sentiment, as was the case among all ancient peoples, have lost all religious significance and obligation, and have given way to the national laws and institutions of such lands and peoples to which the Jews belong by birth and civic relationship.[35]

As examples of laws with no further applicability in the modern age, Holdheim included the biblical distinction between taking interest from an Israelite and from a foreigner and the observance of the dietary laws. The case of lending money at interest demonstrates the difference in approach between the Paris Sanhedrin and the second-generation German reformers. The Paris Sanhedrin had interpreted away the apparent double standard in the biblical regulation of interest. Holdheim acknowledged the double standard but dismissed the offensive biblical laws as no longer valid. On the issue of *kashrut,* Holdheim dismissed the continuing validity of dietary laws on the basis that they hearkened back to a time when Israel saw itself as having a particular theocratic union with God, a conception that was now foreign to Jewish thought; besides, "these laws are particularly prone to continue the differences between them and the other inhabitants."[36] Thus not only marriage and divorce and lending money at interest were, for Holdheim, civil matters, but also such ostensibly religious practices as *kashrut* and the biblical laws of cleanliness, for they were part and parcel of Israel's ancient theocracy.

The chief legal arguments adduced against Holdheim's analysis of Jewish marriage law were twofold. First, although the methods of "acquiring" a wife might be akin to the modes of acquiring property, the legal difference of a marital union was demonstrated by the fact that a man may not dispose of a wife by any means, for example, by gift to another, as he may of personal or real property. Rather, a marital relationship could be terminated only by the issuance of a *get*. Second, if the woman were the husband's property, he could determine what course to pursue in the event of her infidelity. Jewish law, however, requires the termination of the marital union in such a case. Indeed, the woman was to be put to death.[37]

Holdheim's attempt to restrict the scope of the religious realm in Judaism must be understood within the historical context in which he wrote. As has been earlier observed, the activities of the nineteenth-century religious reformers were largely motivated by the desire for political emancipation. In 1842, Bruno Bauer, a Protestant theologian and Hegelian philosopher, published a tract on the Jewish problem, in which he unequivocally pronounced the Jews unfit for citizenship.[38] Holdheim's work was aimed in part at disproving Bauer's allegations.

Bauer characterized the Jews as a nation which, fenced in by its laws, had pressed itself against the wheel of history. As long as the Jew remained a Jew, he could not be fully emancipated: "All assurances of the most enlightened Jew that he is not dreaming of a sovereign nation for 'his people' are illusory however sincerely they may be meant. As long as he wants to be a Jew, he can and must not deny his nature, the exclusiveness, the idea of a special destiny, the Kingdom." *Dina de-malkhuta dina* was thus, for Bauer, an illusory formula because the Jew always remains loyal to "his people." As a case in point, Bauer devotes an entire section to analyzing the pronouncements of the Paris Sanhedrin.[39] He calls the "political-religious" distinction "the lie" and sets out to expose it. Although the Sanhedrin cited the ancient counsel of Jeremiah to "seek the welfare of the city,"[40] it neglected to observe that the city was doomed to destruction. The law of the Jews recognizes One Sovereign and no other. Furthermore, every aspect of life is regarded by the law as religious and there is no independent sphere of civil affairs. The very fact that many important addresses delivered in the Paris Sanhedrin were presented in Hebrew with French translation, reflects the Jews' view that Hebrew is the real and French the offprint, in life as in language.

> It would be fine if the Jew openly declared: "I want—since I wish to remain a Jew—to keep only that much of the Law which seems to be a purely religious element; everything else which I recognize as anti-social I shall weed out and sacrifice." But instead he pretends to himself, and he wants to make others believe that in this distinction between religious and political commands he remains in accord with the Law, that the Law itself recognizes and establishes this distinction. Instead of breaking with a part of the Law he remains a servant of the whole, and as such he must give up that distinction again and alienate himself through his religious consciousness from the real world. Judaism cannot be helped, the Jews cannot be reconciled with the world, by the lie.[41]

Christianity, as the perfection of Judaism, carries to the extreme the opposition of the law to the real world. Christianity knows only nationality rooted in Jesus. Christians, for their own emancipation, must emerge from the barriers of the church. Only when both Christians and Jews give up their special nature will they be able to treat one another as men and mutually enjoy

125

political emancipation in a state freed from the curse of religion. Of course, the Jews' emancipation requires a far greater leap than that of the Christians, for it demands a negation of a negation. The Jew must first negate his particularism by passing through the phase of universal exclusive claims characteristic of Christianity. Only after this step of self-negation could Jews proceed to true emancipation.[42]   Ultimately, the most influential response to Bauer's thesis was that of his friend and former student, Karl Marx.[43] Whereas Bauer sought to purge society of religion, creating thereby a state of spiritually and politically free citizens, Marx rejected the continued existence of the state. For Marx, the state as well as religion had to wither away, in order to permit the return of society to a condition in accord with the true nature of man. The present unnatural bourgeois society was pervaded by the character of Judaism; ridding itself of this enslavement would emancipate mankind: "Let us look at the real Jew of our time; not the Jew of the Sabbath, whom Bauer considers, but the Jew of everyday life. What is the Jew's foundation in our world? Material necessity, private advantage. What is the object of the Jew's worship in this world? Usury. What is his worldly god? Money. Very well then, emancipation from usury and money, that is, from practical, real Judaism, would constitute the emancipation of our time." In Marx's formulation, "Jewish emancipation means, ultimately, the emancipation of humanity from Judaism," which is a system of self-interests.[44] Marx's indictment of capitalist society intertwined with his negative observations on Judaism, was, in the twentieth century, to have a more serious impact on Jewish life than either the essay of Bauer or the treatise of Holdheim.

In an effort to bring some cohesiveness to their activities, twenty-five reformist rabbis held a conference at Brunswick in June 1844.[45] The rabbis so assembled viewed themselves as the heirs of the Paris Sanhedrin.[46] Hence one of the acts of the conference was the endorsement of its predecessor's doctrinal decisions. The difference in the two assemblies, however, is nowhere better manifest than in this endorsement. The rabbis at Brunswick ignored the very careful and deliberate denial of the possibility of *kiddushin* between a Jew and a non-Jew proclaimed by the Paris Sanhedrin and declared: "The marriage of a Jew with a Christian, marriage with adherents of monotheistic faiths in general, is not forbidden, if the laws of the state permit the parents to rear the children of such a union also in the Jewish faith."[47] The reformers at Brunswick purported to be adding the requirement regarding the rearing of children as a stringency to the Sanhedrin's decision, which they interpreted as permitting intermarriage between Jews and monotheists. The nature of the "stringency" is, itself, highly significant. First, it demonstrated the political aspirations underlying the reform activity. State laws forbade the intermarriage of Jews and Christians, a stigma the Jewish reformers wished to erase.[48] That intermarriage was ruled permissible if state law allowed the children of such unions to be raised as Jews suggests that this political concern was more important to the reformers than the issue of whether the child would actually be reared as a Jew. Second, the child's status according to Jewish law was ignored in this declaration.[49] In adopting the balance of the Paris Sanhedrin's decisions, the principle of deferring to state law in all matters except in distinctively religious affairs was specifically affirmed by the Brunswick Conference.[50]

Among the practical reforms agreed upon at the Conference was the elimination of *Kol Nidre* from the Yom Kippur liturgy, along with the declaration that "the oath of a Jew in the name of God is binding without further ceremony."[51] This action was in response to the criticism of non-Jews that the Jews absolved themselves of all oaths on their Day of Atonement and to the centuries-old oath *more Judaica* by which Jews in Europe were required to swear.[52] Again, it was hoped that inner reform would lead to changes in the Jews' political status. Committees were appointed by the Brunswick Conference to report on various liturgical questions,[53] the Sabbath, and marriage law at a conference to be held the following year in Frankfort-on-the Main. In the interim, the Protocol of the Brunswick proceedings was published.

The traditionalist reaction to this conference and the published record of its deliberations came in the form of a book, *Torat ha-Kena'ot*, issued in 1845, containing the letters of the leading European rabbis opposing reformist activity.[54] Jewish "loyalists" were urged to disregard the heretical pronouncements published in the Brunswick Protocol, for the vast majority of their perpetrators were unlearned; one was obliged to "incline after the majority,"[55] and the bona fide rabbis of Germany, France, Italy, Holland, Poland, and Russia all opposed such innovations; the matters concerning which the reformers sought to act were beyond the legislative authority of even a qualified Jewish legal tribunal; and they violated the biblical injunction against adding to or detracting from the law. Samson Raphael Hirsch and numerous other contributors to this work pointed to the conference's misconstruction of the decision of the Paris Sanhedrin regarding intermarriage. The Orthodox respondents praised the Paris Sanhedrin, which, despite the difficult circumstances under which it convened, remained steadfast in affirming Jewish law. Not only was intermarriage with Christians forbidden, declared one rabbi, so was intermarriage with the reformers. One rabbi mockingly asked whether the reformers' position on intermarriage was acceptable to any of the nations whose favor the reformers so dearly sought.[56]

The principal arguments marshaled against recognizing the actions of the reformers were an expression of the continuing sovereignty of the Jewish legal system: because the reformers had violated both procedural and substantive norms of Jewish law, their acts were null. In contrast, the Paris Sanhedrin, although affirming the continuing validity of various details of Jewish law, had, in effect, acknowledged the end of Jewish legal sovereignty. The appeal to the decisions of the Paris Sanhedrin by the opponents of reform is thus an argument in the alternative: even if one posits the end of Jewish legal sovereignty, the specifics which the reformers address are inviolable.

As in *Eleh Divrei ha-Brit*, written one generation earlier, the traditionalists strongly condemned the reformers' rejection of messianic beliefs and affirmed the devotion of God-fearing Jews to the heads of state. They reiterated that the rejection of the notion of the redemption of Israel was heresy and belittled the reformers for their readiness to abandon the fundamental tenets of Judaism to secure political advantage. The elimination of Kol Nidre, it was observed, suggested that heretofore the Jews had been liars but that they were now going to keep their word. If the reformers wished to invoke *dina de-malkhuta dina* in support of their actions, let them recall that this principle was not applicable to matters of *issur ve-hetter*. If they claimed to act by *hora'at sha'ah*,

129

let them remember that this principle permitted the imposition of stringencies by the sages to guard against sin; it did not allow the abolition of existing legal requirements. Let it be known that "their officiation at a *kiddushin* is null and their supervision of a *get* is void, for they do not believe in the words of the sages of Israel who ordered for us laws of marriage and divorce; and one must suspect that they are not in the category 'Israel.'"[57]

A separate response to the Brunswick Conference came in an article by Zachariah Frankel, in his *Zietschrift für Religiose Interessen*.[58] Frankel, whose approach to religious reform had previously been set forth during the second Hamburg prayerbook controversy,[59] denied the authority of a rabbinical conference to institute religious reforms and criticized the insensitivity of the conferees to the religious sentiments of the Jewish people. Frankel's emphasis on the feelings of the Jewish masses toward tradition is a clear expression of the romantic influence that permeated each of the emerging internal approaches to Jewish religious reform and accommodation to the larger society.[60] For Frankel, the Jewish *Volk, Klal Yisrael*, had given meaning to the Divine revelation at Sinai by the laws and traditions of the oral law. Religious tradition continued to be observed and developed by the Jewish people, collectively, and could not be repudiated by an isolated group of rabbis.

Although Frankel criticized the process and measures of the reform conference, he shared with the reformers the view that Judaism had evolved through history. Perhaps expecting that he could serve as a moderating influence on reformist activity, Frankel attended the conference at Frankfort in 1845.[61] This conference, which attracted thirty participants, was largely devoted to the liturgical issues that had been raised at the Brunswick Conference. It was on the question of the subjective necessity of retaining Hebrew as the primary language of Jewish worship that Frankel parted way with the reformers, abandoning the conference on the third day. Thus was born the "positive-historical" school of Judaism, as Frankel termed his approach.[62]

Neither the Frankfort Conference nor the subsequent Breslau Conference, in 1846, addressed the matter of marriage law, which had been referred to a committee chaired by Holdheim at Brunswick.[63] A polemical work, *Responsa to Sinners: Holdheim and His Friends*, took issue with the reformers' proposals to abdicate Jewish law in favor of state law in the area of marriage: "'According to the law of Moses and Israel' we have heard, in connection with *kiddushin*—never have we heard 'according to the law of the King and the manners of the nations'!" Moreover, although a Talmudic principle places marriage under rabbinic jurisdiction, the principle is that people marry subject to the authority of the rabbis, "not by the authority of heretics and nonbelievers such as you!"[64]

As the generation between the Congress of Vienna and the liberal revolutions of 1848 drew to a close, several trends were clear. First, an irreparable breach separated Jewish religious reformers and traditionalists. In the application and extension of *dina de-malkhuta dina*, the limits of traditionalist flexibility had been drawn by the Paris Sanhedrin. For the reformers, Judaism was a religious confession, which had to be purified of its archaic ceremonial and nationalist dross in the modern age. Regarding themselves as the legitimate heirs of Mendelssohn and the Paris Sanhedrin, nineteenth-century reformers struggled to achieve social and political integration into the German states, declaring their exclusive devotion to the fatherland. As Leopold Stein, the reform rabbi of Frankfort, phrased it: "We are Germans and want to be nothing else! We have no other fatherland than the German fatherland, and wish for no other! Only by our faith we are Israelites, in every other respect we belong with devotion to the state in which we live."[65] As invoked by the reformers, *dina de-malkhuta dina* increasingly became an internal sanction for the abdication of Jewish law in all areas of conflict with state law.[66] The state, not Jewish law, was the source of legal authority. In all matters arrogated by the state to its own jurisdiction, Jewish law would yield.

Second, with the breakdown of Jewish autonomy and the challenge of adjustment to nineteenth-century Western society, a variety of religious movements was to characterize Jewish life. Not only the traditional Orthodoxy of pre-Enlightenment Europe, but the neo-Orthodoxy of Samson Raphael Hirsch claimed to be the authentic expression of Judaism. In addition to the organized European reform movement, the positive-historical school of Zachariah Frankel was to be nurtured in the Breslau Theological Seminary and ultimately to give rise to the Conservative Movement in the United States.[67]

Third, notwithstanding the romantic summons of Hirsch to examine Judaism "from within," the critical examination of Judaism had become a significant, independent discipline. Only the future, however, would reveal whether Jewish science was investigating a vital, living tradition or whether, as a contributor to *Der Orient* wrote in 1848, "Our history is concluded and has been absorbed into general history. An autonomous Judaism lives on solely in the synagogue and in the world of learning."[68]

Summary and Conclusions

The period of nearly one century between the Revised Privilege for the Jews of Prussia in 1750 and the revolutions of 1848 was a time of dramatic change in the life of western and central European Jewry. In the transition from corporate community to individual citizen, the principle *dina de-malkhuta dina* was frequently invoked as a means of harmonizing the requirements of religious law with the demands of the state. As with any legal doctrine, it was variously applied by strict constructionists and by more expansive interpreters. Until the modern age, however, all rabbinic interpreters of the principle were in agreement as to the basic source of its authority. Only because Jewish law provided for the recognition of state law in a particular category of cases was there such a concept as *dina de-malkhuta dina*.

During the corporate phase of Jewish life, European Jewry enjoyed wide-ranging judicial autonomy. Under such conditions, the application of *dina de-malkhuta dina* was restricted, in the main, to the limits set out in the Talmud, dating to a time of Jewish autonomy in Babylonia. The principle was applied to matters of taxation and confiscation, defined as *mamona*, and was complemented by the prohibition against resort to non-Jewish tribunals in litigating disputes between Jews.

The principle was not, however, strictly one of accommodation. It also provided a rationale for resistance to the implementation of unjust decrees. Consonant with the general trend toward the acceptance of positive law in the thirteenth and fourteenth centuries, and in response to the reality of the *servi camerae* status to which the Jews had been reduced in the aftermath of the Crusades, the concept of *gezelah de-malkhuta* was significantly diminished. The king's law, whether preserving "good old law," and whether equitable or not, was law, at least in the commercial sphere. Even in this period, however, the basis for extending the principle's application was rabbinic decision. Concomitantly, there was a noticeable decline in the exclusive jurisdiction of rabbinic courts in western Europe; recourse to courts operating under the king's law became more common. In matters of religious prohibition *(issura)*, however, rabbinic jurisdiction remained unchallenged.

With the accelerated erosion of corporate life in the eighteenth century, under the impact of absolutism and enlightenment, even issues treated by Jewish law as *issura* became the subjects of state legislation, and *issura* disputes were brought before state tribunals by Jewish litigants. Moses Mendelssohn, though remaining faithful to the observance of Jewish law, demanded an end to the community's power of excommunication. In effect, he called for an end to all vestiges of Jewish legal autonomy. Moreover, Mendelssohn's distinction between Israel's eternal, ceremonial law and its defunct political constitution was variously interpreted and applied by those who followed him. Whereas traditionalists viewed this distinction as a reaffirmation of the *issura-mamona* categories in the application of *dina de-malkhuta dina*, reformers so extended the political-religious distinction of *Jerusalem* as to justify the abdication of all Jewish practices that conflicted with the norms of the state. They accomplished this end by making the state the ultimate determinant of what was properly within the purview of religious law.

Jews were first accorded equality of citzenship in revolutionary France. Napoleon demanded a clear statement of the Jews' relationship to the state, summoning a Sanhedrin to pronounce upon this subject. Recognizing and accepting the collapse of Jewish legal autonomy, the Paris Sanhedrin asserted only the continued validity of Jewish ritual law, specifically in matters of marriage and divorce. The new definition of synagogue-state relations thus established may be seen as the ultimate stage in a process that began as early as the thirteenth century. Once the absolute power of the king to legislate in the commercial sphere was acknowledged, the abdication of all but ritual jurisdiction was conceivable. The total loss of communal autonomy, however, subjected even the ritual authority of the rabbinate to voluntary compliance by individuals following the French Revolution.

The principle *dina de-malkhuta dina* was frequently invoked in the struggle for political emancipation in Prussia during the first half of the nineteenth century. Religious reformers carried the principle to what they saw as its logical conclusion. Matters involving interpersonal relations, particularly if regulated by the state, were civil *(mamona)*; only the private matter of religious belief was beyond the scope of *dina de-malkhuta dina*. Hence such practices as strict Sabbath observance, dietary restrictions, and special family law usages had no place in Jewish life in the modern state. Such a conclusion, with its legal basis in *dina de-malkhuta dina,* effectively turned Samuel's dictum on its head. It is small wonder that traditionalists responded to this claim with polemics of rage.

The discussions and disputes over the scope of *dina de-malkhuta dina* from 1750 to 1848 reflect the struggle of western European Jewry to accommodate to the twin challenges of emancipation and adjustment. The various approaches that emerged in response to the new reality of Jewish life in postcorporate society have left a legacy to the present day. In this eventful century of transition, the Talmudic dictum *dina de-malkhuta dina* was a factor in Jewish life, the significance of which remains vital to an understanding of Judaism in the modern era.

Abbreviations

AJS Newsletter	Association of Jewish Studies Newsletter
BB	Babylonian Talmud, Tractate Bava Batra
BK	Babylonian Talmud, Tractate Bava Kamma
CCARY	Central Conference of American Rabbis Yearbook
EH	Even ha-Ezer
EJ	Encyclopedia Judaica
Git.	Babylonian Talmud, Tractate Gittin
HJ	Historia Judaica
ḤM	Ḥoshen Mishpat
HUCA	Hebrew Union College Annual
JJS	Jewish Journal of Sociology
JQR	Jewish Quarterly Review
JSS	Jewish Social Studies
Ket.	Babyonian Talmud, Tractate Ketubbot
Kid.	Babylonian Talmud, Tractate Kiddushin
LBIY	Leo Baeck Institute Yearbook
Ned.	Babylonian Talmud, Tractate Nedarim
PAAJR	Proceedings of the American Academy of Jewish Research
REJ	Revue des etudes juives

Abbreviations

Sh. Ar.   *Shulkhan Arukh*
Yad   Maimonides' Code of Jewish Law: *Yad ha-Ḥazakah*
Yev.   Babylonian Talmud, Tractate Yevamot

Notes

Introduction

1. Jer. 29:7.

2. Neh. 9:37. This verse was quoted in the earliest attempt to provide a rationale for the third-century legal dictum *dina de-malkhuta dina* (the law of the kingdom is law). See Simha Asaf, *Teshuvot ha-Geonim* (Jerusalem: Hebrew University ha-Madpis, 1942), sec. 66; Shmuel Shilo, *Dina De-Malkhuta Dina* (Jerusalem, 1974), pp. 44–45.

3. Avot 3:2.

4. Jacob Neusner has suggested that Samuel's dictum emerged out of the favorable situation enjoyed by Babylonian Jewry under Sassanid rule and the apparent friendship between Samuel and the Sassanid ruler, Shapur I (*A History of the Jews in Babylonia*, vol. 2 [Leiden: E. J. Brill, 1966], pp. 64–70). Leo Landman, *Jewish Law in the Diaspora: Confrontation and Accommodation* (Philadelphia: Dropsie College, 1968), pp. 19–22, disputes this view.

5. Ned. 28a; Git. 10B; BK 113a–b; BB 54b–55a.

6. "In modern times, reformist Jewish trends have risen which, *inter alia*, have relied upon the three words *dina de-malkhuta dina* as proof for their tendencies and perspectives.

Notes to Chapter 1

We will not deal with this approach in this study, because our issue is, exclusively, traditional Judaism, and the use of this principle by legal authorities, recognized by observant Jewry, those accepting the 'yoke of heaven'" (Shilo, *Dina De-Malkhuta Dina*, p. 2).

7. As one reviewer of Shilo's work wrote, "It is the task of the historian of any given period to take this vast storehouse of information presented here by Dr. Shilo and place it in its proper perspective" (Jacob Schachter, "*Dina de-Malkhuta Dina*—A Review," *Diné Israel* 7 [1977] : 87).

8. See, e.g., Jacob Katz, *Out of the Ghetto: The Social Background of Jewish Emancipation, 1770–1871* (New York: Schocker, 1978), and Shmuel Ettinger, "The Modern Period," in *A History of the Jewish People*, ed. H. H. Ben-Sasson (Cambridge, Mass.: Harvard University Press, 1976).

9. On the approaches of various Jewish historians to resolving this difficulty, see Michael Meyer, "Where Does the Modern Period of Jewish History Begin?" *Judaism* 24 (1975): 329–38.

10. This process is detailed in Azriel Shoḥet, *Im Ḥilufei Tekufot: Reishit ha-Haskalah be-Yahadut Germania* (Jerusalem: Mosad Bialik, 1960), and is discussed in Chapter 2, below.

11. Salo W. Baron, *A Social and Religious History of the Jews* (Philadelphia: Jewish Publication Society, 1957), 9: v.

Chapter 1

1. BK 113a: *Mishnah:* No money may be taken in change either from the box of the customs collectors or from the purse of tax collectors, nor may charity be taken from them [note: Rashi: *le-fi she-hem shel gezel* (because they [the funds] are stolen)]. *Gemara:* "In the case of customs collectors, why should the dictum of Samuel not apply that the law of the State is law? R. Ḥanina b. Kahana said that Samuel stated that a customs collector who is bound by no limit (is surely not

acting lawfully). At the School of R. Jannai it was stated that we are dealing here with a customs collector who acts on his own authority"; Ned. 28a: *Mishnah:* "One may vow to murderers, robbers and publicans that it [the produce which they demand] is *terumah,* even if it is not, or that it belongs to the royal house, even if it does not. Beth Shammai maintains: one may make any form of vow, excepting that sustained by an oath; but Beth Hillel maintains: even such are permissible. . . . *Gemara:* But Samuel said, *dina de-malkhuta dina.* R. Ḥanina said in the name of R. Kahana in the name of Samuel: The Mishnah refers to a publican who is not limited to a legal due. The School of R. Jannai answered: This refers to an unauthorized collector."

2. BK 113b: *Gemara:* "The above text [BK 113a] (stated): Samuel said 'The law of the State is law.' Said Raba: You can prove this from the fact that the authorities fell palm trees [without the consent of the owners] and construct bridges [with them] and we nevertheless make use of them by passing over them. He, however, said to him: If the rulings of the State had not the force of law, why should the proprietors abandon their right? Still, as the officers do not fully carry out the instructions of the ruler, since the ruler orders them to go and fell the trees from each valley [in equal proportion], and they come and fell them from one particular valley [why then do we make use of the bridges which are thus constructed from misappropriated timber?]. The agent of the ruler is like the ruler himself and cannot be troubled [to arrange the felling in equal proportion], and it is the proprietors who bring this loss on themselves, since it was for them to have obtained contributions from the owners of all the valleys and handed over [the] money [to defray the public expenditure]."

3. BB 54b: *Gemara:* "Rab. Judah said in the name of Samuel: The property of a heathen is on the same footing as desert land; whoever first occupies it acquires ownership. The reason is that as soon as the heathen receives the money he ceases to be the owner, whereas the Jew does not become the owner till he obtains the deed of sale. Hence [in the interval] the land

141

is like desert land and the first occupier becomes the owner (note: he must, however, reimburse the purchaser). Said Abaye to R. Joseph: Did Samuel really say this? Has not Samuel laid down that the law of the Government is law, and the King has ordained that land is not to be acquired save by means of a deed? R. Joseph replied: I know nothing of that. [I only know that] a case arose in Dura di-ra 'awatha in which a Jew bought land from a heathen and another Jew came and dug up a little of it, and when the case came before Rab. Judah he assigned the land to the latter. Abaye replied: You speak of Dura di-ra 'awatha? There the fields belonged to people who hid themselves and did not pay the tax to the King, and the King had ordered that whoever paid the tax should have the usufruct of the field. [Hence, we cannot infer from this that land bought from a heathen is not like desert land.]"

4. BB 55a: "Rabbah said: These three rules were told me by 'Ukba b. Neḥemiah the Exilarch: that the law of the Government is law; that Persians acquire ownership by 40 years' occupation; that if property is bought from the rich landlords who buy up land and pay the tax on it, the sale is valid. This applies, however, only to [land] which is transferred to the landlords on account of the land tax; if [it is sold to them] on account of the poll tax, then a purchase from them is not valid, because the poll tax is an impost on the person."

5. Ibid. Under Jewish law, a purchaser of land must acquire the real estate from an owner who holds title by a legal instrument *(shetar)*. Under Persian law, an owner who held a piece of land for forty years was the presumptive owner, and no legal instrument was necessary to establish his ownership.

6. Git. 10b: *Mishnah:* "All documents which are accepted in heathen courts, even if they that signed them were gentiles, are valid except writs of divorce and emancipation. . . . *Gemara:* (Our Mishnah) lays down a comprehensive rule in which no distinction is made between a sale and a gift. We can understand that the rule should apply to a sale, because the purchaser acquires the object of sale from the moment when he hands over the money in their (the non-Jewish judges)

presence, and the document is a mere corroboration; for if they did not hand over the money in their presence, they would not do injury to themselves (their reputation) by drawing up a document of sale for him. But with a gift (it is different). Through what (does the recipient) obtain possession? Through this document (is it not)? And this document is a mere piece of clay? Said Samuel: The law of the Government is Law. Or if you prefer, I can reply: Instead of 'except writs of divorce' in the Mishnah, read 'except (documents) like writs of divorce.' [I.e., all which in themselves make the transaction effective, such as the record of a gift.]"

7. On the issue of taxation and confiscations during the Gaonic period and their treatment in contemporary responsa, see Jacob Mann, "The Responsa of the Babylonian Geonim as a Source of Jewish History," *JQR* 10 (1919): 123–33.

8. Yitzhak Baer has demonstrated that many aspects of the medieval European *kehillah* have their antecedents in the Second Temple period ("Ha-Yesodot ve-ha-Hathalot Shel Irgun ha-Kehillah ha-Yehudit Biymei ha-Beina'im," *Zion* 15 [1950] : 1–41).

9. On Jewish communal life during the Middle Ages see Israel Abrahams, *Jewish Life in the Middle Ages* (London: E. Goldston, Ltd., 1932), and Salo W. Baron, *The Jewish Community* (Philadelphia: Jewish Publication Society, 1942). On the rabbinic synods and their enactments during the Middle Ages see Louis Finkelstein, *Jewish Self-Government in the Middle Ages* (New York: P. Feldheim, 1964).

10. See H. H. Ben-Sasson, ed., *A History of the Jewish People* (Cambridge, Mass.: Harvard University Press, 1976), pp. 410–41.

11. Robert Chazan, ed., *Church, State and Jew in the Middle Ages* (New York: Behrman House, 1980), pp. 60–62.

12. The privileges accorded the Jews by European rulers were not viewed favorably by the church. Thus, for example, in a letter to King Philip Augustus of France, Pope Innocent III wrote (1205): "It does not displease God, but is even acceptable to Him, that the Jewish dispersion should live and serve

under Catholic kings and Christian princes until such time as their remnant shall be saved, in those days when 'Judah will be saved and Israel will dwell securely.' Nevertheless, such princes are exceedingly offensive to the sight of the Divine Majesty who prefer the sons of the crucifiers, against whom to this day the blood cries to the Father's ears, to the heirs of the crucified Christ" (Ibid., pp. 171–72).

13. The *geonim* were the heads of the academies of Sura and Pumbedita in Babylonia from the end of the sixth to the eleventh centuries. See Introduction, note 2, which cites the one Gaonic responsum that addressed the question of the rationale for *dina de-malkhuta dina*.

14. Rashi, Git. 9b.

15. Maimonides, *Yad*, Gezelah 5:18.

16. Rashbam, BB 54b.

17. Ran, Ned. 28a.

18. Rashba (Solomon ben Abraham Adret, ca. 1235–1310), Yev. 46a.

19. Git. 36b, Yev. 89b.

20. Irving Agus, ed., *Teshuvot Ba'alei ha-Tosafot* (New York: Talpiyot, 1954), no. 12.

21. *Hidushei ha-Ritba* (R. Yom Tov ben Abraham Asbili, ca. 1250–1330), BB 55a.

22. *Aliyyot de-Rabbenu Yonah* (R. Yonah ben Abraham Gerondi, ca. 1200–1263), BB 55a, found in *Shitah Mekubbezet*.

23. *She'elot u'Teshuvot Heishiv Moshe*, Hoshen Mishpat, sec. 90, quoted in Shilo, *Dina De-Malkhuta Dina*, p. 3. Writing of the use of *dina de-malkhuta dina* by rabbinic authorities during the Middle Ages, Salo Baron observed: "*Dina de-malkhuta dina* was more frequently invoked than clarified" (*Social and Religious History of the Jews*, 5: 77).

24. Literally, "early authorities," referring to the rabbinic authorities from the decline of the Babylonian Gaonate (early eleventh century) to the middle of the sixteenth century.

25. Literally, "latter ones," used to designate later rabbinic authorities, as opposed to the *rishonim*.

26. *Sefer ha-Tashbeẓ* (written by R. Simeon ben Ẓemah Duran, 1361–1444), pt. 1, no. 158. According to the opinion that *dina de-malkhuta dina* was based on *hefker bet din hefker*, this conclusion followed of necessity. Similarly, Rashi's explanation of the principle as stemming from the Noahide laws requires this conclusion. For those who saw *dina de-malkhuta dina* as rooted in a contract between the ruler and his subjects, the contract was thought not to extend to religious law, which is outside the realm of the king's interest.

27. *She'elot u-Teshuvot ha-Ritba*, Resp. 53.

28. Maimonides, *Yad*, Gezelah 5:14; *Sh. Ar.*, HM 369:8.

29. *She'elot u-Teshuvot Maharik* (R. Joseph Colon, ca. 1420–80), no. 194.

30. Shalom Albeck, "Dina De-Malkhuta Dina be-Kehillot Sefarad," *Abraham Weiss Jubilee Volume* (New York: Shulsinger Bros., 1964), p. 110.

31. *Ḥidushei ha-Ritba*, BB 55a.

32. Fritz Kern, *Kingship and Law in the Middle Ages*, trans. S. B. Chrimes (Oxford: B. Blackwell, 1939), p. 153.

33. See Shilo, *Dina De-Mulkhuta Dina*, pp. 194–95 and citations.

34. Kern, *Kingship and Law*, p. 184.

35. See Shilo, *Dina De-Malkhuta Dina*, pp. 194–95 and citations.

36. Alfasi was silent on the matter.

37. Shilo, *Dina De-Malkhuta Dina*, pp. 200–201.

38. Maimonides, *Yad*, Gezelah 5:18.

39. BK 113a; Ned. 28a; *Tashbeẓ*, pt. 3, no. 46.

40. BK 113a; Ned. 28a.

41. See, e.g., *Teshuvot Maharam* (Rabbi Meir of Rothenburg, ca. 1215–93), no. 128. In certain cases, taxation beyond ordinary limits was accepted, as, for example, "for great needs," such as financing a war (Haggahot Mordecai, BB no. 659).

42. "In these times, all taxes given to the authorities are considered as ordinary taxes" (*She'elot u-Teshuvot Mahari*

Weil [R. Jacob ben Judah Weil, first half of the fifteenth century], 38. See also, Shilo, *Dina De-Malkhuta Dina*, pp. 206–7. In keeping with earlier authorities, the *Shulkan Arukh* preserved the distinction between justified taxes and confiscations and those without legal justification (*Sh. Ar, HM* 369:6–11).

43. BB 55a; *She'elot u-Teshuvot ha-Radbaz* (Rabbi David ben Solomon ibn Abi Zimra, 1479–1573), pt. 4, no. 54. The elimination of this restriction had already been proposed by the RI (R. Joseph ben Meir ha-Levi ibn Migash, 1077–1141), who held that the prohibition against confiscating land for failure to pay other than the land tax was strictly a function of Persian law. Other kingdoms could legitimately exercise broader confiscatory power. See *Shitah Mekubbezet*, BB 55a. Although a purchaser of confiscated goods defined as *gezelah de-malkhuta* could conceivably have been stripped of his ownership, under Jewish law, the rabbis, operating within the realities of medieval life, sometimes invoked the principle that when A gives up on the possibility of recovering his stolen goods *(ye'ush)* and, subsequently, B lawfully acquires them, B is the bona fide owner. See Shilo, *Dina De-Malkhuta Dina*, p. 279.

44. Baron, *Social and Religious History of the Jews*, 5: 78.

45. Similar limitations were placed upon the benefits an individual could enjoy through a tax exemption granted him by the king: if one Jew were exempt, the tax burden would fall that much more heavily upon his coreligionists in the same locale. The Talmud distinguished between an individual who sought a tax exemption and one who received an unsolicited exemption (BB 55a). Only the latter would enjoy this bounty. Hai Gaon went a step further and looked to the time of the exemption as well as to its initiator. Only if an unsolicited exemption was granted before the tax at issue was levied upon the community could the individual so exempted enjoy the benefit (Joseph Habib, *Nimukei Yosef*, in the name of Hai Gaon). This focus on the time as well as on the initiator of the

exemption was a major element in the rabbinic consideration of the exemption issue in medieval Europe.

46. Kern, *Kingship and Law;* pp. 81–97; quotation on p. 84.

47. Ibid. See e.g., the ruling of Rashba, quoted by Bet Yoseph *Tur* Ḥoshen Mishpat, 26, end.

48. Terumot, 8.4; *Yad,* Yesodei ha-Torah, 5:5.

49. *Bet ha-Beḥira,* Sanhedrin 72b.

50. *She'elot u-Teshuvot ha-Rosh,* 8, 10.

51. Taz, *Sh. Ar.,* Yoreh De'ah 157.8.

52. See 2 Sam. 20.

53. *She'elot u-Teshuvot Zera Emet* 2, 51.

54. Git. 10b.

55. Exod. 21:1.

56. Git. 88b. Compare this with 1 Cor. 6:1–6: "Dare any of you, having a matter against another, go to law before the unjust, and not before the saints? Do ye not know that the saints shall judge the world? and if the world shall be judged by you, are ye unworthy to judge the smallest matters? Know ye not that we shall judge angels? how much more things that pertain to this life? If then ye have judgments of things pertaining to this life, set them to judge who are least esteemed in the church. I speak to your shame. Is it so, that there is not a wise man among you? no, not one that shall be able to judge between his brethren? But brother goeth to law with brother, and that before the unbelievers."

57. The scope of rabbinic jurisdiction in Spain of the Reconquista is discussed later in this chapter. In Moslem lands, Jews enjoyed *dhimmi* (protected) status and were generally free to organize themselves as they wished. Thus the *yeshivot* under Islamic rule continued to exercise the influence they had assumed under pre-Islamic rulers. See Ben-Sasson, ed., *History of the Jewish People,* pp. 423–32. In the Byzantine Empire, Jews continued to be governed by the provisions of the sixth-century Justinian Code, which provided that Jews were free in civil suits against fellow Jews to repair to their own courts upon the mutual agreement of the litigants. R.

147

Isaiah ben Mali of Trani, a twelfth-century Talmudist, criticized Byzantine Jewry both for its laxity in ritual observance and for its general disinclination to consult the rabbis in seeking resolution of disputes (Andrew Sharf, *Byzantine Jewry* [London: Schocken, 1971], pp. 175–77).

58. Finkelstein, *Jewish Self-Government*, pp. 155–56. The "seven elders" were heads of the congregation, sometimes referred to as *parnassim* (Abrahams, *Jewish Life in the Middle Ages*, pp. 68–69). The weapon of excommunication was highly effective because in the corporate society of medieval Europe, it withdrew the banished person from the protection of his corporation. For a description of law enforcement within the Jewish community during the Middle Ages, see Baron, *Jewish Community*, 2:208–45. The Magdeburg Jury Court decisions, documenting thousands of German and central European cases, do not record a single instance of a Jew bringing suit against another Jew in a non-Jewish court (Guido Kisch, "Relations between Jewish and Christian Courts in the Middle Ages," *Louis Ginzberg Jubilee Volume* [New York: American Academy for Jewish Research, 1945], p. 20).

59. *Yad*, Git. 1.5.

60. The Talmud ascribes a series of *takkanot* to Ezra the Scribe (fifth century B.C.E.), (BK 82a).

61. Deut. 17:11.

62. The right of the court to uproot a law of the Torah in matters of civil law.

63. Yev. 90b.

64. See beginning of this chapter.

65. Chazan, ed., *Church, State and Jew*, p. 290.

66. This "discovery" had been acted upon by the Emperor Justinian, who decreed in his Novella 146, enacted in 533: "The Mishnah, or as they call it the second tradition, we prohibit entirely. For it is not part of the sacred books, nor is it handed down by divine inspiration through the prophets, but the handiwork of man, speaking only of earthly things, and having nothing of the divine in it. But let them read the holy words themselves, rejecting the commentaries, and not con-

cealing what is said in the sacred writings, and disregarding the vain writings which do not form a part of them, which have been devised by them themselves for the destruction of the simple." The Novella is quoted in full in James Parkes, *The Conflict of Church and Synagogue* (London: Soncino Press, 1934), pp. 392–93. The Novella further regulated Jewish synagogue practice and belief, as announced in its heading: "A Permission granted to the Hebrews to read the Sacred Scriptures according to Tradition, in Greek, Latin, or any other Language, and an Order to expel from their community those who do not believe in the Judgment, the Resurrection, and the Creation of Angels" (ibid.). On the scope of Novella 146, see Baron, *Social and Religious History of the Jews*, 3:11–15, and Albert Baumgarten, "Justinian and the Jews," *Joseph H. Lookstein Memorial Volume* (New York: Ktav Publishing House, 1980), pp. 37–44. On the changing pattern of Christian polemics against the Jews during the twelfth century, see Amos Funkenstein, "Changes in the Patterns of Christian Anti-Jewish Polemics in the 12th Century," *Zion* 33 (1968): 125–44.

67. On the role of the mendicant orders in the changing attitude toward Jews and Judaism, see Jeremy Cohen, *The Friars and the Jews* (Ithaca: Cornell University Press, 1982).

68. Kern, *Kingship and Law*, p. 71.

69. Finkelstein, *Jewish Self-Government*, pp. 257–58.

70. *She'elot u-Teshuvot ha-RI* (ibn Migash) 122; *She'elot u-Teshuvot Ribash* (R. Isaac ben Sheshet Perfet, 1326–1408), 232.

71. The term "Sanhedrin" is a Hebraized or Aramaized form of the Greek "synedrion" (assembly, governing body) and seems to have been generally adopted as a reference to the Judaean high court toward the end of the Hasmonean period (first century B.C.E.). The term "Great Sanhedrin" is used in the Talmud exclusively in reference to the supreme court in Jerusalem before the destruction of the Second Temple, which sat in the Gazit-chamber of the Temple. It was not applied to the academies of the second century, although they assumed many of the functions of the high court. The special functions

Notes to Chapter 1

of the Great Sanhedrin are enumerated in the Mishnah: "a tribe, a false prophet, or the high priest may not be tried save by the court of seventy-one; they may not send forth the people to wage a battle of free choice save by the decision of the court of one and seventy; they may not add to the city (of Jerusalem), or the courts of the Temple save by the decision of one and seventy; they may not set up Sanhedrins for the several tribes save by the decision of the court of one and seventy; and they may not proclaim (any city to be) an apostate city save by the decision of the court of one and seventy" (M. Sanhedrin 1.5). Although this description seems to reflect political theory as conceived by the sages rather than actual practice, it indicates the view of the national significance of the Sanhedrin in the tradition of the sages. See Sidney B. Hoenig, *The Great Sanhedrin* (New York: Bloch Publishing Co., 1953); Hugo Mantel, *Studies in the History of the Sanhedrin* (Cambridge, Mass.: Harvard University Press, 1961).

72. *She'elot u-Teshuvot ha-Rosh* 17, 8, quoted and translated in Abraham A. Neuman, *The Jews in Spain*, vol. 1 (Philadelphia: Jewish Publication Society, 1942), pp. 138–39.

73. Quoted in Finkelstein, *Jewish Self-Government*, pp. 362–63. The branding of an informer provided for in the Valladolid enactment is an example of a punishment borrowed from the surrounding legal system. It has no precedent in Jewish law.

74. Judicial ordination was thought to have extended in an unbroken chain from Moses to Joshua and onward to the sages of the Sanhedrin. Originally, an ordained teacher personally conferred ordination upon his qualified pupil, but the consent of the *nasi* (patriarch) came to be required after the destruction of the Second Temple. The extinction of *semikhah* is generally associated with the time of Hillel II, in the latter part of the fourth century, though some date it with the end of the Patriarchate in 425, and others set the time as late as the eleventh century, with the end of the Gaonic period. Based upon Maimonides' opinion that "if all the sages in the land of Israel would agree to appoint and ordain judges, then these new

ordinants would be ordained [*semukhim*]," an attempt was made to revive *semikhah* in sixteenth-century Safed. A record of this attempt and the ensuing controversy is preserved in the *Kuntres ha-Semikhah*, written by its chief opponent, Levi ibn Habib (Ralbah). On the sixteenth-century *semikhah* controversy, see Jacob Katz, "Mahaloket ha-Semikhah Bein Rabbi Ya'akov Berab ve-ha-Ralbah," *Zion* 16 (1951): 28–45.

75. As the Rashba explained: "We have no power lawfully to try cases of capital punishment, nor to impose any fines, except as an emergency measure (Rashba, 5, 238). In every generation, the prerogative is given to the courts to punish and to smite offenders who would destroy the 'fences' set up by the people. And any rabbi who exercises this right, may blessings come upon him (Rashba, 4, 264)" (trans. in Neuman, *Jews in Spain*, p. 143).

76. BT Sanhedrin, 46a; Yev., 90b; PT Hagiga 11b.

77. As the paradigm example of the suspension of legal norms by the exercise of *hora'at sha'ah*, Yev. 90b cites the action of Elijah the Prophet in offering a sacrifice at Mount Carmel, an act forbidden by the Torah (sacrifices were to be offered only at the Temple in Jerusalem).

78. On the laws regulating *hora'at sha'ah*, see Maimonides, *Yad*, Sanhedrin 24:4–10. See also *Encyclopedia Talmudit*, 8:521–27.

79. Thus, for example, the Valladolid enactments specified the death penalty for those who defamed fellow Jews before the Gentile authorities. This, above all other legal infractions, could result in dire consequences for the Jewish population.

80. Ps. 119:126. This verse is quoted as the basis for permitting the writing of texts of Aggada, although the oral tradition was not to be recorded: "Since it cannot be dispensed with, we say, 'when it is time to work for the Lord, they break the law'" (Git. 60a). In Jewish law, the rise of extralegal royal power dates to the first century B.C.E. During the Herodian period, the Sanhedrin was decimated by the king, who transformed the judicial tribunal into a Hellenistic privy council. As such, it ceased to operate by biblical prescription and functioned

instead by royal fiat. Thus, for example, when Hyrcanus denied allegedly treasonous correspondence with the Nabataean king, Herod "showed his letter to the Sanhedrin, and put the man to death, immediately" (Josephus Flavius, *Antiquities of the Jews*, 15.2, trans. William Whiston [New York: W. Borradaile, 1824]). Josephus records of Herod's rule: "the kingdom remaining was entirely in Herod's own power, and there was nobody remaining of such dignity as could put a stop to what he did against the Jewish laws" (Ibid., 15.7. end). The absolute power of the royal courts of the king of Israel, so established, became a recognized part of Jewish law. As codified by Maimonides: "Although Kings of the House of David . . . are judged [by the Sanhedrin] in a suit against them, the Kings of Israel . . . are not judged, because they do not submit to the discipline of the Torah. [To sit in judgment on them] might lead to untoward consequences" (Maimonides, *Yad, Judg.* 2:5).

81. James Fleming, Jr., and Geoffrey C. Hazard, Jr., *Civil Procedure*, 2d ed. (Boston: Little, Brown, 1977), pp. 8–20. On Jewish law and equity see Moshe Silberg, *Talmudic Law and the Modern State* (New York: Burning Bush Press, 1973), pp. 93–130.

82. Neuman, *Jews in Spain*, p. 147.

83. *She'elot u-Teshuvot ha-Rashba* 2, 19; 4, 92; 7, 142, trans. in Neuman, *Jews in Spain*, p. 151. It was, however, common practice among the Jews of Spain to draw up notarial documents—promissory notes, deeds of sale, wills, and testaments—in the general courts, before the public notary, and documents so executed were accorded recognition by the rabbis (Rashba, 3, 15).

84. The desire for strengthened autonomy and the fear of injustice from non-Jewish courts were, no doubt, also motivating factors in the rabbinic enactment against repairing to these tribunals. "The attitude of Jewish law toward a different legal system is determined, first and foremost, by its basic objective of safeguarding its own continued existence and flowing therefrom, autonomous Jewish jurisdiction with all that it

entails" (Menachem Elon, ed., *The Principles of Jewish Law* [Jerusalem: Keter Publishing House, 1975], p. 33).

85. He further required that it be known that the judges and witnesses did not accept bribes and that the document at issue record that the witnesses saw the exchange of money (Maimonides, *Yad,* Hilkhot Malve ve-Loveh 27:1).

86. The procedure involved in executing the documents, however, had to comport with Jewish legal requirements (*She'elot u-Teshuvot ha-Ramban,* 52).

87. *Ḥidushei ha-Ramban,* Git. 10b. See also, Shilo, *Dina De-Malkhuta Dina,* pp. 326–27. In the Spain of Naḥmanides' day, the royal officials who exercised judicial authority regularly consulted the rabbis in their adjudication of Jewish cases. It was also the established norm that matters litigated between Jews, even if brought before non-Jewish royal officials, were resolved by the canons of Jewish law. See Neuman, *Jews in Spain,* pp. 152–53, and citations.

88. See Ben-Sasson, *History of the Jewish People,* pp. 478–81.

89. Chazan, ed., *Church, State and Jew,* pp. 63–64.

90. *Piskei ha-Rosh,* Git. 1:10.

91. Rema, *Sh. Ar.,* ḤM 68:1.

92. Ben-Sasson, ed., *History of the Jewish People,* pp. 646–47.

93. The question of the applicability of *dina de-malkhuta dina* to a Jewish sovereign in the land of Israel was a theoretical issue debated by the *rishonim.* Although examination of this debate is outside the scope of the present work, the issue is important today, in light of the developing relations between church and state in modern Israel. The subject has been addressed in numerous articles. For a bibliographical listing, see Naḥum Rakover, *Oẓar ha-Mishpat* (Jerusalem: Harry Fishel Institute, 1975), p. 227. See also Shilo, *Dina De-Malkhuta Dina,* pp. 99–108.

Chapter 2

1. On the history of this period, see Matthew S. Anderson, *Europe in the Eighteenth Century, 1713–1783* (London: Oxford University Press, 1976); Max Beloff, *The Age of Absolutism, 1660–1815* (New York: Hutchinson's University Library, 1954); Paul Hazard, *The European Mind, 1680–1715* (Cleveland: World Publishing Co., 1969); John B. Wolf, *The Emergence of the Great Powers, 1685–1715* (New York: Harper, 1963).

2. Jews were legally prohibited from owning land and were tolerated only as long as they performed a useful economic function. Hence their situation necessitated the active employment of investment funds. See Jacob Katz, *Tradition and Crisis* (New York: Free Press of Glencoe, 1961), pp. 47–48.

3. It was customary among the various court Jews to arrange marriages between their children in order to extend their business dealings and to enhance their mutual wealth and prestige (Selma Stern-Taeubler, "The First Generation of Emancipated Jews," *LBIY* 15 [1970]: 4); see also Stern-Taeubler, *The Court Jew* (Philadelphia: Jewish Publication Society, 1950). Kinship connections were also an important factor in the commercial success of Amsterdam's Sephardic Jews during the seventeenth century (Daniel M. Swetchinski, "Kinship and Commerce: The Foundations of Portuguese Jewish Life in Seventeenth Century Holland," *Studia Rosenthaliana* 15 [1981]: 52–74).

4. The Jewish community of Berlin, for example, grew from 50 families in 1670 to nearly 4,000 people in 1770 (Isaac Barzilay, "The Background of the Berlin Haskalah," in *Essays in Honor of Salo W. Baron* [New York: Columbia University Press, 1959], p. 190). In all of Germany, the number of Jews at the end of the eighteenth century has been assessed at 175,000 and, in Austria, at 70,000. The total number of Jews in Holland was about 50,000 and, in France, about 40,000 (Katz, *Out of the Ghetto*, pp. 9–10).

5. It was far simpler for the absolute state to curb Jewish

autonomy than to curtail the privileges of other classes. The latter were supported by historical rights, but the autonomy of the Jews had depended from the outset on the will of the ruler (Katz, *Tradition and Crisis*, p. 249).

6. Quoted in Shohet, *Im Hilufei: Tekufot*, p. 75.

7. Ibid., pp. 72–75. Shohet attributes this disaffection, in part, to the paucity of qualified judges in Ashkenaz, a fact recognized by the rabbinate of the time. The decline of the rabbinate in Germany in the aftermath of the calamities of the fourteenth century has been noted in Chapter 1. See also Finkelstein, *Jewish Self-Government*, p. 81.

8. Shohet, *Im Hilufei Tekufot*, pp. 75–88. Of course, the definition of a ceremonial or ritual matter was not always clear. On the herem see Katz, *Tradition and Crisis*, p. 249.

9. Trans. in Jacob R. Marcus, *The Jew in the Medieval World* (Cincinnati: Union of American Hebrew Congregations, 1938), p. 96.

10. Ironically, it was during the wars of Leopold I that trade in military supplies and war financing became a virtual Jewish monopoly. See Raphael Straus, "The Jews in the Economic Evolution of Central Europe," *JSS* 3 (1941): 15–40. The edict of Frederick William can be found in English translation in Marcus, *The Jew in the Medieval World*, pp. 75–79.

11. Heinz M. Graupe, *The Rise of Modern Judaism: An Intellectual History of German Jewry, 1650–1942* (New York: R. E. Krieger Publishing Co., 1979), pp. 93–94; Marcus, *The Jew in the Medieval World*, pp. 88–89; Selma Stern-Taeubler, "The Jews in the Economic Policy of Frederick the Great," *JSS* 11 (1949): 133.

12. The memoirs of Glueckel of Hameln reflect the fundamentally traditional world view of even the most "worldly" German Jews of the seventeenth century (*Memoirs of Glueckel of Hameln*, trans. Marvin Lowenthal [New York: Harper and Bros., 1932]). Shohet has demonstrated that elements of the dissolution of traditional Jewish society are discernible by 1700, but Katz has correctly noted that the evidence marshaled by Shohet does not reflect a reshaping of values but,

rather, a variation of the old system, justified within traditional norms (Katz, *Out of the Ghetto*, pp. 34–37).

13. Mendelssohn (1729–86), who popularized the philosophy of Leibniz, earned a reputation as one of the leading lights of the German Enlightenment. Though an observant Jew, he did not address himself to issues of Jewish philosophy early in his career. He became a symbol to both non-Jewish intellectuals and the *maskilim* of the virtuous, enlightened Jew. See Alexander Altmann, *Moses Mendelssohn* (University, Ala.: University of Alabama Press, 1973).

14. Moses Mendelssohn, *Jerusalem and Other Jewish Writings*, trans. A. Jospe (New York: Schocken, 1969), p. 61.

15. Ibid., p. 89. This passage was a precursor of the "mission of Judaism" concept, which was to find abundant expression in nineteenth-century Jewish thought. In a letter to Herz Homberg, Mendelssohn expressed the opinion that were the Jews to integrate fully with the Christians the world would regress to barbarism within fifty years (Mendelssohn, *Gesammelte Schriften*, vol. 5 [Leipzig: Brockhaus, 1844], pp. 669–70).

16. Mendelssohn, *Jerusalem*, pp. 102–5. On Mendelssohn's political theory and his analysis of symbolic actions, see Amos Funkenstein, "The Political Theory of Jewish Emancipation from Mendelssohn to Herzl," *Jahrbuch des Instituts für Deutsche Geschichte* 3 (1980): 15–22.

17. Baruch Spinoza, *Tractatus Theologica-Politicus*, trans. R.H.M. Elwes (London: Bohn's Philosophical Library, 1883), p. 72.

18. Ibid., p. 59.

19. Mendelssohn, *Jerusalem*, p. 47.

20. See, in this regard, Amos Funkenstein, Review of Alexander Altmann's *Moses Mendelssohn*, *AJS Newsletter*, June 1974, pp. 14–15.

21. Moses Mendelssohn, *Gesammelte Schriften*, vol. 19 (Stuttgart: F. Frommann, 1974), pp. 156, 168. Regarding Mendelssohn and the Schwerin burial controversy, see Altmann, *Mendelssohn*, pp. 288–95. On the eighteenth-century *halak-*

hic debate over the burial issue generally, see Moshe S. Samet, "Halakha ve-Reforma" (Ph.D. dissertation, Hebrew University, 1967), pp. 76–172.

22. Mendelssohn, *Gesammelte Schriften*, 19:110. *Jerusalem* received an enthusiastic response in Christian intellectual circles, to whom it was primarily addressed. Mirabeau proclaimed that Mendelssohn's work "deserves to be translated into all languages," and Kant wrote to the author: "I consider this book the promise of a great reform which will, to be sure, only gradually and slowly be realized—not, however, in regard to your nation alone, but for all other peoples" (quoted in Israel Zinberg, *A History of Jewish Literature*, trans. B. Martin [New York: Ktav Publishing House, 1977], 8:57). On Mendelssohn's political philosophy, see Nathan Rotenstreich, "Mendelssohn's Political Philosophy, "*LBIY* 11 (1966): 28–41.

23. Mendelssohn, *Jerusalem*, p. 104.

24. On the *Toleranzpatent* and its implications for the status of the Jews, see Katz, *Out of the Ghetto*, pp. 162–64. For the text of the primary provisions of the edict see Raphael Mahler, *Jewish Emancipation: A Selection of Documents* (New York: American Jewish Committee, 1941), pp. 18–20. The *Toleranzpatent*, along with the appearance of Nathan Lessing's *Nathan der Weise* (1779) and Christian Wilhelm von Dohm's *Ueber die buergerliche Verbesserung der Juden* (1781, 1783), sparked high hopes of political emancipation among the *maskilim*.

25. It has been suggested that Wessely did not fully comprehend the meaning and implication of his remarks in *Divrei Shalom ve-Emet*. See Moshe Pelli, *Naphtali Herz Wessely's Attitude toward the Jewish Religion as a Mirror of a Generation in Transition* (Beersheva: University of the Negev, 1971), p. 19.

26. David Friedlander, *Lesebuch für Judische Kinder*, re-edited by Moritz Stern (Berlin: Soncino, 1927).

27. In a letter to Herz Homberg, Mendelssohn expressed the view that only the acquisition of secular learning and the

creation of cultural values of general importance by the Jews would result in a new attitude toward them (Mendelssohn, *Gesammelte Schriften*, 5: 680).

28. Regarding the educational program of the first generation *maskilim*, see Isaac Barzilay, "The Ideology of the Berlin Haskalah," *PAAJR* 25 (1956): 33–37. When these efforts proved futile, the *maskilim* endeavored to impress upon state authorities the great differences between enlightened and Orthodox Jews. See Barzilay, "Background of the Berlin Haskalah," p. 197 and citations.

29. Much has been written about Jewish family life and its legal regulation during the premodern period. See, for example, Abrahams, *Jewish Life in the Middle Ages;* Ze'ev W. Falk, *Jewish Matrimonial Law in the Middle Ages* (London: Oxford University Press, 1966); Avraham Freimann, *Seder Kiddushin ve-Nissu'in Aharei Hatimat ha-Talmud* (Jerusalem: Mosad ha-Rav Kook, 1945); Asher Gulak, *Yesodei ha-Mishpat ha-Ivri: Torat ha-Mishpaha ve-ha-Yerusha,* vol. 3 (Berlin: Dvir, 1922).

30. Upon the act of *kiddushin*, the woman *(arusa)* is regarded as a married woman for all purposes, as a matter of biblical law. She may not marry any other man, except upon divorce or the death of her affianced husband. The man is also prohibited from taking an additional wife, in consequence of the eleventh-century *herem de-Rabbenu Gershom* (see note 45 below). During the period between *kiddushin* and the second phase of marriage, *nissu'in,* cohabitation is prohibited.

31. Kid. 2a.

32. The man says, "Behold you are reserved unto me by this money (or ring), according to the law of Moses and Israel." The woman's acceptance of the *kesef* signifies her assent to the union.

33. Kid. 12b.

34. This principle was enunciated in connection with a case in which a man divorced his wife and then spent a night with her in a hotel. The School of Hillel ruled that since "no man engages in sexual intercourse for licentious purposes,"

kiddushin was effectuated by this cohabitation and a second divorce was required to terminate the renewed state of marriage (Git. 81a–b). Although many authorities generalized the principle to all instances of cohabitation, Maimonides restricted it to limited fact situations (Maimonides, *Yad*, Geirushin 10:19).

35. Tosefta, Ket. 4:9; BB 48b. The formula also reflects the cardinal principle that there can be *kiddushin* only between two Jews.

36. Yev. 90b; Ket. 3a; Git. 33a, 73a; BB 48b.

37. Since the man had to be the owner of the money, its expropriation rendered the *kiddushin* void.

38. *Sefer ha-Tashbez,* pt. 2, Resp. 5.

39. *Ozar ha-Geonim,* Ket., *Teshuvot,* Resp. 60.

40. *She'elot u-Teshuvot Rashba,* pt. 1, Resp. 1206.

41. *She'elot u-Teshuvot ha-Rosh,* 35.1.

42. Ket. 2a. The parties could agree upon a lesser period of time. A *Ketubbah* is a document recording the financial obligations of a husband toward his wife, in consequence of their marriage. The *arus* could choose to execute such a document during the *kiddushin* period.

43. Deut. 24:1. Based upon the phrase a "document [literally, "book"] of cutting off," it was held that the terms of the bill of a divorce had to sever the spousal relationship completely. See *Sh. Ar., EH* 137. The Bible does not require the woman's consent to a *get,* but the herem *de-Rabbenu Gershom* imposed this requirement. See note 45.

44. The *Mishnah* specifically prohibits effectuating a divorce in non-Jewish courts (Git. 10b).

45. The subsequent marriage of the wife was considered adultery. Although biblically the husband was permitted to marry more than one woman, an eleventh-century rabbinic ordinance known as the herem *(ban) de-Rabbenu Gershom* (so called after Rabbenu Gershom Me'or ha-Golah, ca. 960–1028, under whose authority the ordinance was issued) prohibited bigamy.

46. *Gillui arayot* refers to biblically prohibited unions

which are punishable by death or excision, such as marriages between parties related to each other within the prohibited degrees of kinship enumerated in Lev. 18:6ff.

47. Yad, Ishut 1.6; Sh. Ar., EH 15.1, 18.

48. The issue of concubinage and the legal relationship arising therefrom was also a matter of rabbinic discussion. See Louis Epstein, "The Institution of Concubinage among the Jews," PAAJR 6 (1934–35): 153–88.

49. A married woman separated from her husband who may not, by Jewish law, remarry. According to Jewish law, a marriage can be terminated only by the death of a spouse or by the husband's issuing his wife a get (bill of divorce). Thus if the husband disappears and there is no positive proof of his death, or if he refuses to issue a get, a woman assumes the status of an agunah.

50. She'elot u-Teshuvot Ribash, no. 6.

51. The required transfer and declaration before competent witnesses were lacking. The parties' intention was implicit in their being married in the church.

52. In general, Jewish law tends to relax certain stringencies to avoid condemning a woman to the status of an agunah. This tendency can be found in the Talmud (Yev. 88a, 122a). Ironically, denying the validity of a marriage performed other than by "the law of Moses and Israel" would leave the woman in a preferable legal position to that which she would occupy were the validity of the marriage affirmed.

53. Terumat ha-Deshen, pt. 1, Resp. 109.

54. She'elot u-Teshuvot Darkhei Noam, EH, Resp. 46.

55. See Freimann, Seder Kiddushin ve-Nissu'in, pp. 346–55, and citations.

56. A Hanover merchant, Mayer Michael-David, told his fellow Jewish traders in Amsterdam in 1773 that the difference between Amsterdam and London on the one hand and the German states on the other was as that between heaven and hell (I. Schoffer, "The Jews of the Netherlands: The Position of a Minority through Three Centuries," Studia Rosenthaliana 15 [1981]: 90).

57. A sense of the power of the Sephardic kahal of Amster-

dam may be discerned from the Del Sotto affair of 1670. This episode erupted in the aftermath of the death of the childless Jacob Delmonte (alias Jacob del Sotto), senior patriarch of an extensive and wealthy family. The *parnassim* of the Sephardic community expected to be nominated as executors of a substantial bequest on behalf of the *kahal*'s poor in the decedent's will. Upon requesting to see the will, the *parnassim* were told that there was none—the deceased, while on his deathbed, had ordered his bookkeeper to throw it into the fire. The *parnassim* did not take kindly to this account and excommunicated the Delmonte heirs. For a brief time, the heirs formed their own *minyan* and established their own cemetery. Apparently, however, the effect of the excommunication, which cut off communication with all members of the religious community except for immediate family, weighed heavily upon the Delmontes, for in 1671 they settled their dispute with the *parnassim* by turning over large sums of money to be used for poor relief (Swetchinski, "Kinship and Commerce," pp. 70–73). Although Swetchinski cities this incident as an example of the power of a strong, commercially active clan pitted against the outside world, the facts suggest another reading of the episode: notwithstanding the power and influence of a very successful late seventeenth-century Amsterdam clan, the Sephardic *kahal* was sufficiently strong to impose and enforce its will.

58. The responsum is found in a collection of responsa of the Portuguese *kahal*, *She'elot u-Teshuvot Etz Ḥaim* 4:447–50, and is quoted in Freimann, *Seder Kiddushin ve-Nissu'in*, pp. 362–64.

59. By Dutch law, the man would be punished for his bigamy, but the first marriage would (as by Jewish law) remain valid. The second wife would be free to marry.

60. *She'elot u-Teshuvot Ribash*, no. 6. In a dictum, the responsum suggested that if it were possible to trace Yoḥanan's whereabouts and obtain a *get*, it would be desirable, "for it is unseemly that it be said that a married woman goes [from a relationship] without a divorce."

61. A summary of the *Ehepatent* can be found in Freimann,

Seder Kiddushin ve-Nissu'in, p. 312. The regulations did not provide for Jewish marriage in a proceeding outside rabbinic supervision, so the issue of the validity of civil marriage, absent *kiddushin*, did not arise under the *Ehepatent*.

62. Ezekiel Landau, *Das mosaisch-talmudische Eherecht* (Leipzig, 1900), translated to Hebrew by Z. Scheinblum, *Sefer Ḥukei ha-Ishut al Pi Dat Moshe ve-ha-Talmud* (Munkacz: Cohen and Fried, 1902). Page references herein refer to the Hebrew translation.

63. The *Ehepatent* declared that a marriage between a Christian and a person of any other religion was null and void. See ibid., pp. 5–12. Landau further affirmed that only a properly executed *get* can function to effectuate a divorce (ibid., pp. 9, 12).

64. Deut. 13:1.

65. While acknowledging the legitimacy of the *ḥerem de-Rabbenu Gershom*, Landau noted that, despite the prohibition against bigamy, a second marriage was legally effective until terminated by divorce. He did not specify that a bigamist was constrained to divorce his second wife, nor did he suggest that violation of the *Ehepatent* might result in a forced *get* (Landau, *Sefer Ḥukei ha-Ishut*, p. 9).

66. Ibid., pp. 10–11, 16.

67. In addition, Joseph II began drafting Jews for transport service, and in 1793 Francis II of Austria instituted compulsory army service for all citizens, including Jews. Rabbi Landau is known to have addressed the first Jewish recruits with tears in his eyes (Katz, *Out of the Ghetto*, p. 249, n. 12). An address to Jewish draftees into the Austrian army appeared in *Ha-Measef*, 1788, urging them to "serve the Lord through His commandments in the days of respite and to serve the Kaiser at the time of war and battle" ("Toldot ha-Zman," *Ha-Measef* [Berlin, 1788], p. 334).

68. Eliezer Fleckeles, *Teshuvah Me-Ahavah*, pt. 1, Resp. 116.

69. Maimonides, *Yad*, Hilkhot Ishut 4.14.

70. Landau, whose tract had assumed that the *Ehepatent*

included *kiddushin*, had not gone so far as to suggest that a violation of its terms would necessitate a *get*. See Fleckeles, *Teshuvah Me-Ahavah*.

71. Ibid.

72. *Takkanot ha-Kahal*, ordinances enacted by the community, were a common legislative instrument in Jewish life from the tenth century onward. For a description of the sources, scope, and procedural aspects of this authority, see Menachem Elon, *Ha-Mishpat ha-Ivri*, 2 vols. (Jerusalem, 1977), 1:558–630. For the text of the proposal, see *She'elot u-Teshuvot Hatam Sofer*, EH, Resp. 108.

73. Pursuant to the principle *Kol ha-mekadesh a-da'ata de-rabbanan mekadesh*.

74. *Ozar ha-Geonim*, Ket., Teshuvot, Resp. 60.

75. Rosh, 35.1.

76. Rashba, 1, 1206.

77. Tashbez, pt. 2, Resp. 5.

78. If the *kiddushin* were, for some reason, valid, and, nonetheless, the woman were free to marry another man, the second union would be adulterous and any children born therefrom would be *mamzerim*. See Tashbez, pt. 2, Resp. 5.

79. Rema, Sh. Ar., EH 28.21.

80. See Freimann, *Seder Kiddushin ve-Nissu'in*, pp. 316–19.

81. *She'elot u-Teshuvot Hatam Sofer*, Even ha-Ezer, pt. 1, Resp. 108–9. He suggested, rather, that measures be taken to encourage the "daughters of Israel" not to enter into *kiddushin* contrary to state law. Sofer, perhaps, alludes to this in his comment, "The decree is liable to be annulled" (ibid., p. 109). The Napoleonic approach to the relationship between the Jews and the state is discussed in Chapter 3.

82. See note 43; *She'elot u-Teshuvot Rabbi Akiva Eger*, no. 83.

83. See note 43. A similar case was referred to Rabbi Pinhas Horowitz (1730–1805) of Berlin. The issue before him was whether a *get* was effective before the severance of the marital union "according to their practice." Rabbi Horowitz ruled

that the *get* alone was sufficient to terminate the marriage according to Jewish law because from the husband's viewpoint it fully severed the relationship (*She'elot u-Teshuvot Givat Pinḥas*, Resp. 32).

84. Quotation from *She'elot u-Teshovot Ḥatam Sofer*, ḤM, 142. With regard to wills, Jewish law distinguishes between three different testamentary forms, each defined by the circumstances under which it is executed. These are the gift of a healthy person, the gift of a critically ill person, and a gift in contemplation of death (i.e., the gift of a healthy person who faces imminent, possibly fatal, danger). Since there are biblical provisions governing the order of succession (Num. 27:8–11; Deut. 21:16–17), a healthy person wishing to give his property to a person other than his legal heir must divest himself of ownership so that the property will not pass according to the biblical laws of succession. This is accomplished by donating the property to the intended beneficiary by way of a gift, while retaining the usufruct until death. A critically ill person can bequeath his property by either oral or written instruction and can retract his will verbally or in writing. The will of a critically ill person is automatically revoked upon the testator's recovery from illness. The rules regulating the disposition of property by a healthy person in contemplation of death are identical to those governing the gift of a critically ill person. See Shmuel Shilo, "Wills," in *EJ*, 16:519–30 (Jerusalem, 1971). Since the instructions of a critically ill person or of a healthy person in contemplation of death are considered to be of immediate force and effect, any document recorded in connection therewith is merely evidentiary; hence all authorities would agree that it could be recorded in a non-Jewish court. See *Sh. Ar.*, ḤM 253:32.

Chapter 3

1. The term "nation" was used in the eighteenth century as a reference to "ethnographic units with precise

characteristics acquired from experience" (Jacob Katz, "Die Entstehung der Judenassimilation in Deutschland und deren Ideologie," in Katz, *Emancipation and Assimilation* [Farnborough: Gregg International Publishers, 1972], p. 208, quoted in Graupe, *Rise of Modern Judaism*, pp. 86–87).

2. Population data taken from Robert Anchel, *Les Juifs de France* (Paris: J. B. Janin, 1946), p. 235. There was also a small Jewish population in Paris, which included both Sephardic and Ashkenazic Jews.

3. Henri II had issued letters patent in 1550, based upon the economic usefulness of the "marchands portugais," and Louis XIV had issued a new series of letters patent in 1656. On the early history and privileges of the Portuguese nation in France, see Frances Malino, *The Sephardic Jews of Bordeaux* (University, Ala.: University of Alabama Press, 1978), pp. 1–26. Incorporation as the Portuguese nation not only allowed the Sephardic Jews open religious expression but also enabled them to regulate their own commercial affairs.

4. Ibid., p. 24. The Bordeaux community maintained strict scrutiny over marriages. By communal enactment, parental consent as well as permission of the nation, represented by its leadership, were required to effectuate *kiddushin*. The "Registry of the Deliberations of the Portuguese Nation of Bordeaux" includes the record of a case considered in 1783, in which a couple married without the necessary authorization and the *kiddushin* was declared null and void. The *bet din* declared that even if all of the formalities of the *kiddushin* had been properly performed, violation of the local *takkanah* rendered the marriage a nullity (Simon Schwarzfuchs, ed., *Le registre des deliberations de la nation Juive Portugaise de Bordeaux* [Paris: Fundaçao Calouste Gulbienkian Centro Cultural Portugues, 1981], pp. 540–44).

5. Haim Joseph David Azulai, *Sefer Ma'agal Tov ha-Shalem* (Jerusalem: Mekize Nirdamim, 1934), pp. 115–16. Azulai's account of the Jews of the Bayonne area was somewhat more positive (ibid., pp. 110–13).

6. "Because of our great sins, they study only Bible in the

165

Talmud Torah. They [the community leaders] don't want Rashi taught, because he relates midrashim and the interpretations of our Sages of blessed memory. They don't even want Maimonides [taught]. Woe to the eyes which behold this" (ibid., p. 114). The Talmud Torah also offered classes in French and arithmetic.

   7. A census of Alsatian Jews, taken in 1784, showed approximately twenty thousand Jews living in 182 communities. By the treaty of Cateau-Cambrésis (1559) France was permitted to occupy Metz, Toul, and Verdun. French jurisdiction over these areas, as well as over Alsace, was confirmed by the treaty of Westphalia in 1648. In 1697, by the treaty of Ryswick, France acquired Strasbourg. Finally, Lorraine was annexed in 1766. The autonomous Ashkenazic Jewish communities were regarded as official corporations by the judicial and administrative bodies of the French government. Not only were decisions affecting the Jews posted on synagogue doors, but copies of general laws were sent by the authorities to the Jewish communities (Zosa Szajkowski, *Franco-Judaica* [New York: American Academy for Jewish Research, 1962], p. 15). In 1777, representatives of the Alsatian nation met in Nidernai and enacted a number of *takkanot*. These included a definition of the role and powers of the syndics, a statement of various tax obligations devolving on community members, and a prohibition against marriages without rabbinic authorization. The syndic was empowered, with the accord of a tribunal of three rabbis and the approval of the government intendant, to pronounce a *ḥerem* against a Jew who violated religious norms. The published *takkanot* requested that any dishonest business dealings of a Jew be reported to the syndics so that such conduct could be punished and stopped. See Isidore Loeb, "Les Juifs à Strasbourg depuis 1349 jusqu'a La Révolution," *Annuaire de la Société des Etudes Juives*, vol. 1 (Paris, 1883), pp. 181–91.

   8. On the economic status of the Ashkenazim in France, see Zosa Szajkowski, *The Economic Status of the Jews in Alsace, Metz and Lorraine* (New York: Editions Historiques Franco-Juives, 1954), p. 57 and passim.

9. A reflection of anti-Jewish feeling in the "provinces" can be seen in the petition of the Jews of Alsace, December 1771, that the right to judge cases of usury be taken from the local judges and reserved to the royal law courts, functioning under the jurisdiction of French law (ibid., p. 115). It was not uncommon for anti-Jewish leaders to serve as judges in cases involving Jews. The most notorious example is that of Judge Hell, instigator of the "false receipts" debacle.

10. Quoted in Arthur Hertzberg, *The French Enlightenment and the Jews* (New York: Columbia University Press, 1968), p. 181; see also p. 182. The attempt of the "enlightened" Jews to distinguish themselves has already been seen with reference to the Berlin *maskilim* (Chapter 2, n. 28).

11. Christian Wilhelm von Dohm, *Concerning the Amelioration of the Civil Status of the Jews*, trans. Helen Lederer (Cincinnati: Hebrew Union College–Jewish Institute of Religion, 1957), p. 80.

12. Dohm commented that a cessation of oppression would bring about more positive results vis-à-vis the Jews than in the case of the gypsies, who were also the objects of ameliorative legislation by Joseph II, because the Jews were not strangers in the states in which they dwelled. This assessment of the relative merits of the Jews and the gypsies was not universally shared. A slogan of the time suggested that it would be easier to integrate the gypsies than the Jews because the former were merely uneducated whereas the latter were maleducated (H. D. Schmidt, "The Terms of Emancipation, 1781–1812," *LBIY* 1 [1956]: pp. 28–29).

13. This argument is reminiscent of a similar claim made by Simcha Luzzatto in his tract *On the Jews of Venice*, published in Italian in 1638. See the Hebrew edition of this work, *Ma'amar al Yehudei Venezia* (Jerusalem: Mosad Bialik, 1950), pp. 83–84. Menasseh ben Israel invoked the same argument in promoting the readmission of Jews to England, 1649–56. See Paul Mendes-Flohr and Jehuda Reinharz, eds., *The Jew in the Modern World: A Documentary History* (New York: Oxford University Press, 1980), p. 10. Likewise, the philosopher John Toland, citing Luzzatto, advanced this notion in his *Rea-*

sons for Naturalizing the Jews of Great Britain and Ireland
(1714). With reference to Toland's treatise, Shmuel Ettinger
has observed that "there is hardly an argument that appeared
afterwards in Jewish apologia in the eighteenth and nineteenth centuries which was not mentioned by Toland" ("The
Beginnings of the Change in the Attitude of European Society
toward the Jews," *Scripta Hierosolymitana* [Jerusalem: Magnes Press, 1961], 7:218).

14. Mendelssohn objected to Dohm's stand on Jewish
juridical autonomy in his preface to the German translation of
Menasseh ben Israel's *Vindiciae Judaeorum* (1782). A considerable portion of Mendelssohn's *Jerusalem*, subtitled *A
Treatise on Ecclesiastical Authority and Judaism*, is devoted
to arguing against the coercive power of any church.

15. Dohm, *Concerning the Amelioration of the Civil Status
of the Jews*, p. 69.

16. Quoted in Mendes-Flohr and Reinharz, eds., *Jew in the
Modern World*, p. 37.

17. Ibid., p. 38.

18. Hence the census of 1784, the tally of which was, no
doubt, low.

19. On the letters patent of 1784, see Anchel, *Juifs de
France*, pp. 213–33, and Zosa Szajkowski, "The Jewish Problem in Alsace, Metz, and Lorraine on the Eve of the Revolution
of 1789," *JQR* 44 (1953–54): 223–37.

20. The subject was in keeping with the concern for social
betterment which occupied enlightened intellectuals of the
time. The subject for the Metz Society's prize in 1786 was how
to make illegitimate children more useful to the state
(Hertzberg, *French Enlightenment and the Jews*, p. 329). For a
summary of the various positions of the essayists, see ibid.,
pp. 334–38.

21. Abbé Henri Grégoire, *An Essay on the Physical, Moral
and Political Reformation of the Jews* (London: C. Forster,
1791), pp. 150, 165, 194. To facilitate the conversion of the
Jews, Grégoire saw nothing wrong in imposing missionary
sermons upon them: "To obligate Jews to receive instruction is

not obliging them to abjure their religion; and I am inclined to believe, that to compel them to hear some discourses is not contrary to the rights of humanity" (ibid., p. 191).

22. The edict, which applied to those "who do not profess the Catholic religion," was interpreted to include exclusively Protestants.

23. On the Sephardic position before the Malesherbes commission, see Zosa Szajkowski, "Mishlahoteihem shel Yehudei Bordeaux el Va'adat Malesherbes ve-el ha-Aseifa ha-Le'umit," *Zion* 18 (1953): 35–38, 56–59; and Malino, *Sephardic Jews of Bordeaux*, pp. 27–39.

24. Although the report is not extant in its original form, an analysis of it remains in the writings of the Abbé Grégoire. See Maurice Liber, "Les Juifs et la convocation des Etats Généraux," *REJ* 65 (1913): 161–212.

25. As late as April 1790, Berr Isaac Berr, the syndic of the Jewish community of Lorraine, published a pamphlet suggesting that the National Assembly grant the Ashkenazim all rights with the exception of holding public office, with the Jews retaining full communal autonomy (Hertzberg, *French Enlightenment and the Jews*, p. 348).

26. Malino, *Sephardic Jews of Bordeaux*, p. 45.

27. Maurice Liber, "Les Juifs et la convocation des Etats Généraux," *REJ* 65 (1913): 184.

28. Malino, *Sephardic Jews of Bordeaux*, p. 48.

29. On the history of the slogan "a nation within a nation," see Katz, *Emancipation and Assimilation*, pp. 47–76.

30. On the case of the false receipts, see Szajkowski, *Economic Status of the Jews*, pp. 123–40. At the outbreak of the Revolution, the debts had not yet been paid off.

31. Malino, *Sephardic Jews of Bordeaux*, p. 48.

32. Schwarzfuchs, *Le registre*, pp. 578–79.

33. Resolution of September 28, 1791, quoted in Simon Schwarzfuchs, *Napoleon, the Jews and the Sanhedrin* (London: Routledge & Kegan Paul, 1979), p. 11.

34. Letter of Berr Isaac Berr to his brethren, 1791, in Diogene Tama, *Transactions of the Parisian Sanhedrin*, trans.

F. D. Kirwan (London, 1807; rpr. Farnborough, 1971), pp. 15–16.

35. Sinzheim (1745–1812) was a grandson of Abraham Sinzheim, rabbi in Manheim early in the eighteenth century, and the brother-in-law of the Alsatian community leader Cerf Berr. He conducted a *yeshiva*, established by Cerf Berr, in Bischeim until he was forced to flee to Strasbourg during the Revolution. The alliance among scholarship, wealth, and community leadership, often cemented by marriage, was characteristic of European Jewish society. An excellent treatment of the hierarchy of functions in Jewish society of this period can be found in Katz, *Tradition and Crisis*, pp. 199–209. The *Memoirs of Glueckel of Hameln* also reflect this social system.

Furtado (1756–1817) was the son of Portuguese Marranos. After his father's death in the Lisbon earthquake, his mother moved to London, where she returned openly to Judaism. She settled eventually in Bordeaux, where Furtado was educated. Furtado became prosperous through dealings in property and was active in the political affairs of the Portuguese nation.

36. Introduction to David Sinzheim, *Yad David* (Jerusalem: Machon Yerushalayim, 1976), trans. in Schwarzfuchs, *Napoleon, the Jews and the Sanhedrin*, p. 18.

37. Zosa Szajkowski, "Jewish Religious Observance during the French Revolution of 1789," *YIVO Annual of Jewish Social Science* 12 (1958–59): 212–13, 215.

38. On the fate of synagogues during the Revolution, see Zosa Szajkowski, "Synagogues during the French Revolution of 1789–1800," *JSS* 20 (1958): 215–29.

39. On the issue of Jewish communal debts, see Zosa Szajkowski, *Autonomy and Communal Jewish Debts during the French Revolution of 1789* (New York, 1959).

40. Not until 1802 were rabbis forbidden by government order to perform religious marriage ceremonies for couples who had not been married by a civil proceeding (A. E. Halphen, *Recueil des lois concernant les Israelites depuis la Revolution* [Paris, 1851], p. 15).

41. Zosa Szajkowski, "Marriages, Mixed Marriages and

Conversions among French Jews during the Revolution of 1789," *HJ* 19 (1957): 42.

42. Zosa Szajkowski, "French Jews in the Armed Forces during the Revolution of 1789," *PAAJR* 26 (1957): 143.

43. In Russia, too, albeit not by reason of equality of citizenship, Jews were to be conscripted into the army during the first half of the nineteenth century. Austria had begun to draft Jews independent of French influence (see Chapter 2, n. 67).

44. *Zera Emet*, pt. 3, no. 32.

45. An encirclement, either by walls or wires, meeting certain specifications, within which carrying on the Sabbath is permissible.

46. At the same time, Rabbi Ishmael received a second inquiry from the Mantua community, also emerging from the Jews' newly acquired citizenship status. Two Jews were appointed to the City Council. The problem that arose was their participation in a celebration on the Sabbath which would have necessitated their vehicular conveyance. After citing the *halakhic* strictures against riding on the Sabbath, Rabbi Ishmael observed that prohibitions could not be cast aside because of government association except in the limited instance of a rabbinic ordinance which, at the time of its enactment, provided for such an exception (*Zera Emet*, pt. 3, no. 33).

47. Sofer, whose conservative stance has been earlier encountered, was to emerge as the leading traditionalist authority in the struggle against religious reform (see Chapter 5). From 1806 until his death in 1839, he served as rabbi in Pressburg, then the most important Jewish community in Hungary. On the life and thought of Moses Sofer, see Jacob Katz, "Kavim le-Bibliographia shel ha-Ḥatam Sofer," *Studies in Mysticism and Religion Presented to Gershom Scholem* (Jerusalem: Magnes Press, 1967), pp. 115–61.

48. *Likkutei She'elot u-Teshuvot Ḥatam Sofer* (Pressburg, 1864), Resp. 29. For a summary of responsa on military service written during the Middle Ages, see Y. Z. Kahana, "Sherut ha-Ẓava be-Sifrut ha-Teshuvot," *Sinai* 23 (1948): 129–34.

49. Exod. 21:16.

50. See Kahana, "Sherut ha-Zava be-Sifrut ha-Teshuvot," pp. 129–61, and Sheldon Zimmerman, "Confronting the Halakha on Military Service," *Judaism* 20 (1971): 204–12.

51. The Ancona chronicle appears in Baruch Mevorach, *Napoleon u-Tekufato* (Jerusalem: Mosad Bialik, 1968), pp. 17–36.

52. A report in the Paris *Moniteur Universel*, 3 Prairial of the year 7 (May 22, 1799), announced Napoleon's intention to reestablish the ancient Jerusalem. Napoleon purportedly issued a letter to the Jewish nation proposing that the Jews join with him in freeing their land from the Turks. Franz Kobler, *Napoleon and the Jews* (New York: Schocken, 1975), is devoted almost entirely to establishing the authenticity of a certain document, allegedly a copy of this proclamation. For arguments challenging its authenticity, see Schwarzfuchs, *Napoleon, the Jews and the Sanhedrin*, pp. 24–27.

53. On the social problems impeding the Jews' occupational change, see Katz, *Out of the Ghetto*, pp. 178–83.

54. France did not have a law fixing the rate of interest on loans until September 3, 1807. Until then, there was no legal definition of what constituted usury. See Schwarzfuchs, *Napoleon, the Jews and the Sanhedrin*, p. 45.

Chapter 4

1. On the administrative and legal reforms of Napoleon, see Robert B. Holtman, *The Napoleonic Revolution* (Philadelphia: Lippincott, 1967), pp. 72–98.

2. Quoted in J. Christopher Herold, *The Mind of Napoleon* (New York: Columbia University Press, 1955), p. 103.

3. Quoted in Holtman, *Napoleonic Revolution*, p. 130.

4. On Napoleon's relations with the church, see ibid., pp. 121–38.

5. Schwarzfuchs, *Napoleon, the Jews and the Sanhedrin*, p. 45. Schwarzfuchs' recent book offers the best account of the subject of any published work.

6. Poujoul, "Quelques observations concernants les Juifs en général, et plus particulièrement ceux d'Alsace, pour fixer l'attention du Gouvernment sur la legislation des differens peuples à leur égard, sur leurs moeurs et habitudes, et sur les mesures qui pourraient etre convenables d'adopter dans la circonstance actuelle" (Paris, 1806), summarized in Schwarzfuchs, *Napoleon, the Jews and the Sanhedrin*, pp. 34–37. Poujoul noted that he had sent two copies of his work to the emperor.

7. Quoted in Herold, *Mind of Napoleon*, p. 111.

8. The text of Napoleon's decree can be found in his *Correspondance* (Paris, 1863), 12: 411–12, no. 10291, and in English translation in Simeon J. Maslin, *Selected Documents of Napoleonic Jewry* (Cincinnati: Hebrew Union College–Jewish Institute of Religion, 1957), Document I-A.

9. "Les premiers pas de la nation Juive vers le bonheur sous les auspices du grand monarque Napoleon;" Hebrew trans. in Baruch Mevorach, *Ha-Yehudim Taḥat Shilton Napoleon*. Internal publication of the Hebrew University (Jerusalem, 1970), pp. 129–32.

10. See Jacob R. Marcus, "Reform Judaism and the Laity: Israel Jacobson," *CCARY* 38 (1928): 386–498. Brunswick became a part of the kingdom of Westphalia, governed by Napoleon's brother Jerome, 1807–13.

11. Although it cannot be proved that Napoleon read Jacobson's work, it has been suggested that his call for a Sanhedrin to give supreme religious authority to the decisions of the Assembly of Notables was influenced by this volume (ibid., p. 416; Katz, *Out of the Ghetto*, pp. 139–40). Such a conclusion, though not impossible, is not necessary. Napoleon's inclination to revive classical usages has already been observed in his appointment of "High Priests of the Jewish Nation." Moreover, the assembly, in its response to question 8, referred to the Sanhedrin of old and its supreme jurisdiction.

12. Napoleon, *Correspondance*, 12:571–72, no. 10537. The questions are found in ibid., p. 572, no. 10538. The translation herein is taken from Schwarzfuchs, *Napoleon, the Jews and the Sanhedrin*, pp. 56–57.

13. The traditional Ashkenazims' opinion of Furtado and the Portuguese Jews became apparent to the commissioners. Chancellor Pasquier, in his memoirs, recorded: "It soon became clear that the Portuguese Jews were suspect to all their coreligionists who considered them as apostates. President Furtado was more suspect than anyone else. They seemed to believe that he was connected with his religion only by the feeling of human respect which allows one to leave the religion in which one was born only when moved by the strongest of convictions. Now this was not Furtado's outlook: philosophical indifference was the foundation of his opinions. The rabbis of Alsace, and those of the former Comtat of Avignon [a Papal province which had become a part of France], whose knowledge brought them to the forefront, said of their president that visibly he had learned the Bible only in Voltaire" (*Mémoires du Chancelier Pasquier* [Paris, 1893], 1: 276, trans. in Schwarzfuchs, *Napoleon, the Jews and the Sanhedrin*, pp. 64–65).

14. Tama, *Transactions of the Parisian Sanhedrin*, p. 132. Molé added, "As to us [the commissioners], our most ardent wish is to be able to report to the Emperor, that, among individuals of the Jewish persuasion, he can reckon as many faithful subjects, determined to conform in every thing to the laws and to the morality, which ought to regulate the conduct of all Frenchmen" (ibid., pp. 132–33).

15. The notion that the Jews' character had become corrupted as a result of oppression has been seen earlier as a hallmark of Enlightenment apologetics. As a representative of the Portuguese nation before the Malesherbes commission, nearly two decades earlier, Furtado had sought to separate discussion of the legal status of the Sephardim from that of the Ashkenazim. Now, although the summoning of the assembly stemmed from circumstances in Alsace, it seemed clear that the emperor intended to deal with the "Jewish problem" as a whole. Furtado was obliged to present a united Jewish position.

16. Tama, *Transactions of the Parisian Sanhedrin*, pp. 149–50.

17. See Chapter 1, n. 26.

18. Mark 12:17. See Mendelssohn, *Jerusalem*, p. 104.

19. See, e.g., Tama, *Transactions of the Parisian Sanhedrin*, pp. 144, 159.

20. Early during the proceedings, there was some discussion about the relative weight to be accorded the rabbis' opinions. It was determined that the principle of "one man, one vote" should apply, the rabbis' further influence being limited to moral suasion (ibid., pp. 142–44).

21. N. M. Gelber, "La police autrichienne et le Sanhedrin de Napoleon," *REJ* 83 (1927): 138–40.

22. See Chapter 2, n. 45.

23. The response of the assembly acknowledged that state law prohibited the rabbis from imparting the matrimonial benediction absent a prior state decree but did not indicate what the Jewish legal status of such *kiddushin* would be.

24. Tama, *Transactions of the Parisian Sanhedrin*, pp. 153–54.

25. Chapter 2.

26. *Sh. Ar.*, Even ha-Ezer 137, 143. In keeping with the attempt at simplicity, the answer neither cited the chapter of the *Shulkhan Arukh* to which it referred nor gave great detail on the principle at issue.

27. Chapter 2, n. 83.

28. The response avoided any statement about the independent validity of a state-issued divorce.

29. The responses of Rabbi Ishmael are in Mevorach, *Napoleon u-Tekufato*, pp. 107–20.

30. An indication of the high regard in which Rabbi Ishmael was held is discernible in a letter written by Rabbi Israel Carmi of Reggio, who, in extolling the legal scholarship of David Sinzheim, wrote that he was almost of an equal stature to Rabbi Ishmael (October 7, 1806, reprinted in ibid., p. 103).

31. On the historical development of the principle that "the gentiles of our day are not idolators," see Jacob Katz, "Shlosha Mishpatim Apologeti'im be-Gilguleihem," *Zion* 23–24 (1958–59): 186–93.

32. Kid. 68b. This Talmudic passage also applies the pro-

hibition against mixed marriage to unions with non-Jews in general, not merely with the seven Canaanite nations.

33. Tama, *Transactions of the Parisian Sanhedrin*, p. 155.

34. This conclusion was based *sub silentum* on the principle "yisrael af al pi she-ḥata yisrael hu" (Sanhedrin 44a).

35. Tama, *Transactions of the Parisian Sanhedrin*, p. 156.

36. Mevorach, *Napoleon u-Tekufato*, pp. 110–13.

37. Tama, *Transactions of the Parisian Sanhedrin*, pp. 171–72, 180.

38. Mevorach, *Napoleon u-Tekufato*, p. 115.

39. Tama, *Transactions of the Parisian Sanhedrin*, p. 195.

40. Mevorach, *Napoleon u-Tekufato*, p. 116.

41. Tama, *Transactions of the Parisian Sanhedrin*, p. 197.

42. Deut. 23:20–21. In the case of loans at interest to Jews, a special legal form was required, by which the lender shared in the borrower's enterprise *(hetter iskah)*.

43. A letter from a traditionalist observer to an Alsatian cantor in Bohemia reported on Sinzheim's role in the assembly's deliberations: "There were great quarrels between them, because there were present—on account of our faults—a great number of bad and so-called modern Jews, who were ready—God forbid, to abrogate a part [of the law] but the honorable Chief Rabbi Sinzheim intervened and vowed: no dot over an i will be taken from our religion" (Gelber, "La police autrichienne," p. 142; trans. in Schwarzfuchs, *Napoleon, the Jews and the Sanhedrin*, p. 66).

44. The "confessionalization" of Judaism by the assembly has, understandably, subjected its work to harsh criticism by nationalist Jewish historians. Thus, for example, Simon Dubnow wrote: "After starting out by compromise and servility, the assembly kept on sliding downhill. And when it came to the second group of questions—dealing with the compatibility of civic patriotism and the Jewish national feeling— servility passed beyond all bounds" (*History of the Jews*, trans. Moshe Spiegel, vol. 4 [South Brunswick, N.J.: T. Yoseloff, 1971], p. 552).

45. Tama, *Transactions of the Parisian Sanhedrin*, pp.

224–25. The high hopes generated by Napoleon extended to the belief in some quarters that the Temple might be soon rebuilt. Thus it is reported that Rabbi Raphael ha-Cohen (1723–1804) devoted his last years to the study of the Talmudic Order Kodashim, dealing with the priestly service and sacrificial cult, so that he would be prepared to carry out the duties of the priesthood in the rebuilt Temple (Elon, *Ha-Mishpat ha-Ivri*, 1:68–70, esp. n. 14). Napoleon's enemies, too, noticed the Jews' favorable impression of the French emperor. In a report to his superior, Count Stadion, Metternich wrote: "The Israelites of all lands are looking towards this Messiah who seems to be freeing them from the yokes under which they find themselves" (September 24, 1806, quoted in Gelber, "La police autrichienne," p. 136).

46. Tama, *Transactions of the Parisian Sanhedrin*, p. 245. On August 23, Napoleon had sent a directive to his minister of the interior, Champagny, instructing him to convene a "Grand Sanhedrin" and indicating to him the substance of its desired decisions. Among Napoleon's expectations was that the Sanhedrin would recommend mixed marriages and that it would declare that no more than one-half of the Jews drafted could buy their way out of service. The Sanhedrin's decisions would "compose a second body of legislation for the Jews which, while conserving the essential character of that of Moses, will adapt itself to the current situation of the Jews, to our morals and to our customs." An English translation of Napoleon's letter to Champagny may be found in Maslin, *Documents of Napoleonic Jewry*, pp. 6–12, Document I–B. For the further guidance of his commissioners and Council of State, Napoleon sent a second letter, dated November 29, relating to the Sanhedrin. He advised that it was essential for the Sanhedrin to begin its work "by declaring that there are, in the laws of Moses, religious provisions and political provisions; that the religious provisions are immutable but that this does not apply to the political provisions which are susceptible of modification" (ibid., p. 16). Napoleon had evidently been impressed with the language of the assembly's preamble and

wanted the political-religious distinction to be affirmed by the Sanhedrin as a doctrinal decision. Thus the terminology of Mendelssohn was adopted by the greatest monarch of Europe in the process of confessionalizing Judaism. This letter further expressed the desire that one out of every three marriages of Jews be to a Christian, so that "the blood of the Jews will cease to have any unique character" (ibid., p. 21). Napoleon added a personal view that "it is wrong to say that the Jews are only degraded in those places where they are persecuted; in Poland, where they are necessary to fill the place of the middle class of society and where they are esteemed and powerful, they are no less vile, dirty, and given to all those customs of the basest dishonesty" (ibid., p. 22). The full text of Napoleon's letter in English translation can be found in ibid., pp. 16–23, Document I–C.

47. Tama, *Transactions of the Parisian Sanhedrin*, p. 272. Despite the assembly's assertion that the Jews of France and Italy had no ties with their coreligionists in foreign lands, the invitation to participate in the Sanhedrin was directed to Jewish communities throughout the Western world. This invitation, surely instigated by Napoleon, reflects his continuing image of French Jewry as part of an alien international element. Ultimately, there were but two small "foreign" delegations to the Sanhedrin's proceedings, one from Amsterdam and one from Frankfort, both of which areas were under Napoleonic domination. These delegations were permitted to address the Sanhedrin at the conclusion of its deliberations and duly affirmed its doctrinal decisions. A letter was received by Furtado from the rabbi of one community outside French control, Aaron Chorin of Arad (Hungary), who was to become an active and prolific advocate of Jewish reform in the years ahead. Chorin expressed the hope that the assembly would use its rightful authority as a Jewish synod to purify the Jewish religion and requested that he be sent copies of its discussions and decisions. This letter is in the Themanlys Archives in Jerusalem; a microfilm is on file in the Central Archives for the History of the Jewish People, Jerusalem, HM24.

48. This consistorial plan was akin to that which regulated Protestant churches in France. The text of the plan may be found in Tama, *Transactions of the Parisian Sanhedrin*, pp. 285–92. Many of its provisions, such as those regulating the qualifications of rabbis and the doctrines to be preached, were similar to the articles regulating the Catholic and Protestant churches in France. In the case of the rabbinate, however, there was no provision for state-paid salaries.

49. The use of the term *nasi* was in keeping with the attempt to model the Paris Sanhedrin on the ancient Sanhedrin of Jerusalem. Similarly, the members were seated in a semicircle, according to age.

50. A French text of the decisions and the accompanying speeches may be found in Diogene Tama, *Collection de procés-verbaux et decisions du Grand Sanhédrin* (Paris, 1807). I am indebted to Simon Schwarzfuchs for providing me with a copy of this text. In addition, the Central Consistory published an official text of the decisions, in French and Hebrew, in Paris in 1812. The Hebrew text has been reprinted in Mevorach, *Napoleon u-Tekufato*, pp. 88–101.

51. See note 46.

52. A prayer composed by David Sinzheim and recited during the opening session of the Paris Sanhedrin, February 9, extolled Napoleon, who had thought "to gather us in an assembly of seventy-one as the number of the Great Sanhedrin, and he called us, from his mouth, by this glorious name" (Mevorach, *Napoleon u-Tekufato*, pp. 102, 90). Clearly, Sinzheim and the other rabbis of the assembly did not see themselves as reconstituting the Sanhedrin of old.

53. Ibid., p. 92.

54. This approach was in keeping with the thinking of Ezekiel Landau, who had addressed the issue one generation earlier.

55. Mevorach, *Napoleon u-Tekufato*, p. 96.

56. See the side-by-side French-Hebrew edition of the Sanhedrin's decisions issued by the Central Consistory, *Décisions doctrinales du Grand Sanhédrin* (Paris: Sétier fils, 1812), p. 47.

57. The Sanhedrin did not deal with the issue of rabbinic jurisdiction, questions 7 through 9 of the assembly's agenda, because this matter was covered in the consistorial plan.

58. Tama, Collection de procés-verbaux, pp. 78–88; quotation on p. 82. These passages obviously refer to the pronouncements on mixed marriage, polygamy, and the need to secure a civil decree of marriage and divorce. Sinzheim's rationale for requiring a civil marriage or divorce decree—"for the sake of peace"—bears out the possibility that a failure to comply with this requirement might not invalidate the religious decree.

59. Ibid., pp. 83, 92. This is, again, reminiscent of the contract theory of dina de-malkhuta dina. No less an orthodox authority than the Ḥatam Sofer shared Sinzheim's view of the work he had performed in shaping the responses of the assembly and the Paris Sanhedrin. In eulogizing Sinzheim upon his death in 1812, Sofer compared him to Joseph, who had represented his people before Pharaoh without compromising his faith: "During his lifetime he was honored and was very close to the monarchy in Paris; he was asked a number of questions and knew how to answer his questioners. He was great and much honored in the eyes of the emperor and his ministers, and they honored him greatly when he passed away, as is well known. Nevertheless, he was greatly respected by the Jews and busied himself all his life with the study of the whole Talmud a number of times" (David Sinzheim, Minḥat Ani [Jerusalem: Machon Yerushalayim, 1974], trans. in Schwarzfuchs, Napoleon, the Jews and the Sanhedrin, 116).

60. See note 46. The French text of these instructions is in Napoleon, Correspondance, 12:582–85, no. 11320.

61. Quoted in Schwarzfuchs, Napoleon, the Jews and the Sanhedrin, p. 101.

62. Tama, Collection de procés-verbaux, p. 200.

63. In a personal letter to Napoleon, Furtado gave thanks to the emperor, declaring: "Paris will become for us what Jerusalem was for our ancestors in the beautiful days of its glory . . . Israelites in our Temples, French among our fellow

citizens, this is who we are" (quoted in Malino, *Sephardic Jews of Bordeaux*, p. 103).

64. English translations of these decrees may be found in Maslin, *Documents of Napoleonic Jewry*, Documents 1–D, 1–E, and 1–F.

65. Furtado, who, in the aftermath of the assembly's dismissal became aware of the exceptional measures being drafted for the regulation of French Jewry, wrote to the Italian deputy of the assembly, Formiggini, expressing his concern over Napoleon's plans. An example of the naive view of Napoleon, which some Jews continued to hold, is contained in Formiggini's reply: "I believe despite everything that these laws are utterly contrary to the will and thoughts of the emperor. I am certain that the emperor will not permit these steps; to the contrary, perhaps he will be angry at those who have worked in this path" (Yosef Sierra, "Beḥinot Shonot shel Da'at ha-Kahal ha-Yehudit be-Italia al ha-Sanhedrin shel Napoleon," in *Hagut Ivrit be-Europa*, ed. Menaḥem Zohari and Arie Tartakover [Tel Aviv: Yavneh, 1969], p. 360).

66. The decisions of the Sanhedrin were affirmed by the Reform rabbinical conference held in Brunswick in 1844.

67. Leon Lecestre, *Lettres inédites de Napoleon I*, vol. 1 (Paris, 1897), pp. 158–59.

68. The first two volumes of *Sulamith* (Leipzig-Dessau, 1806–9) bore the subtitle *A Periodical to Further Culture and Humanity in the Jewish Nation;* the third volume (Cassel, 1810) changed the phrase *Jewish Nation* to *Among the Israelites.* Starting with the proceedings of the assembly and the Paris Sanhedrin, the term "Israelite" came to be the expression of preference among Western Jews. It seemed to be devoid of the national connotation which the term "Jew" carried, and its biblical background was divorced from the image of the ghetto Jew.

69. *Sulamith* 3 (1810): 303, trans. in W. Gunther Plaut, *The Rise of Reform Judaism* (New York: World Union for Progressive Judaism, 1969), pp. 29–30.

70. The disciples of Mendelssohn, among whose number

Jacobson counted himself, had abandoned their predecessor's allegiance to Jewish observance. What remained of his legacy was accommodation to the European environment. Thus, for example, David Friedlander, who was to propose accepting a modified form of Christianity as a means of obtaining political emancipation, had his tombstone inscribed: "True disciple and friend of the philosopher Moses Mendelssohn" (Michael Meyer, *The Origins of the Modern Jew* [Detroit: Wayne State University Press, 1967], p. 84). Mendelssohn's own descendants were all baptized within two generations.

71. Mendel Steinhardt, *Divrei Iggeret* (Roedelheim: Wolf Heidenheim, 1812), Preface.

72. Indeed, David Friedlander made known his dissatisfaction with what he perceived to be the far too modest program of reform contemplated by the Westphalian consistory (Marcus, "Reform Judaism," p. 434).

73. Steinhardt, *Divrei Iggeret*, p. 1a.

74. Depending upon which text of the Sanhedrin's response one reads, the French or the Hebrew (*Décisions doctrinales*), soldiers are released from religious obligations either during the term of their service or during time of war. In either case, the leniency is restricted to soldiers.

75. The Central Consistory in Paris wrote to Jacobson, expressing surprise that such an action had been taken without soliciting the counsel of other Jewish authorities (Marcus, "Reform Judaism," p. 459).

76. Prayers invoking God's wrath upon the Gentiles, Steinhardt alleged, were both inappropriate and dangerous (*Divrei Iggeret*, p. 12a). Among the measures taken to promote decorum were the recitation of the mourner's *kaddish* in unison (ibid., Resp. 7) and the waving of the *lulav* by the officiant only during Tabernacles (Resp. 5).

77. The procedure whereby the *levir* indicates his refusal to marry his brother's widow, thereby enabling her to marry someone other than himself.

78. Marcus, "Reform Judaism," pp. 453–55.

79. In France the consistorial system survived Napoleon.

The Central Consistory was recognized by the Bourbon regime as an official body.

80. See Chapter 5.

81. See Cecil Roth, *The History of the Jews of Italy* (Philadelphia: Jewish Publication Society, 1946), pp. 406–20.

82. Extracts of the question and response may be found in A.N.Z. Roth, "Bein Yehudim le-Goyim be-Italia be-Reishit ha-Meah ha-19," in *Hagut Ivrit be-Europa*, ed. Zohari and Tartakover, pp. 361–64. The fact that this *halakhic* inquiry was put to Sinzheim by the traditionalist Viterbo further attests to the high regard in which Sinzheim was held by his Orthodox contemporaries well after his service in the assembly and Paris Sanhedrin. Not only did the traditionalists honor him, he was also praised in the pages of the reformist *Sulamith* 1 (1806): 183–84.

83. Roth, "Bein Yehudim," pp. 362–63. Viterbo noted that he was prodded for an opinion by one of the "saving remnant of the leaders of the nation of God" (ibid., p. 362). Reformist tendencies were not absent in Italy, as shown by the appearance of a work by Aaron Fernando of Leghorn in 1814 calling for the abrogation of most Jewish ceremonial law (Roth, *History of the Jews of Italy*, pp. 444–45). The final quotation is in Roth, "Bein Yehudim," p. 363.

84. Roth, "Bein Yehudim," p. 364.

85. The letter from the Italian consistory of Cassal was dated April 30, 1810. The response of the Central Consistory, on Sinzheim's signature, may be found in microfilm copy in the Central Archives for the History of the Jewish People in Jerusalem, HM1063. It has also been reprinted in Simon Schwarzfuchs, "Correspondance du Consistoire Central," *Michael* 1 (1972): 129–30.

86. The Paris Sanhedrin had carefully avoided direct comment on the independent validity of the civil divorce, but it had affirmed unequivocally the need to secure a *get*, in its pronouncements.

87. Response to Question 2.

88. Dubnow, *History of the Jews*, pp. 570–71.

89. This group sent representatives to the Paris Sanhedrin.

90. Dubnow, History of the Jews, p. 572. The issue of early burial was a symbol among the maskilim of Jewish enlightenment. Thus the Society of Friends, an association of maskilim organized in Berlin in 1792, sought, among other things, to impose its wish not be be buried immediately upon the local burial society (chevrah kadishah). It accomplished this objective by appealing to the authorities to force the chevrah kadishah to permit the enlightened free choice in the matter of their own burial and by then hiring the poorer members of the burial society to carry out their wishes (Katz, Out of the Ghetto, p. 151).

91. On the Dutch Jewish consistory and the subsequent Jewish organizational structure in the Netherlands, see J. Michman, "The Conflicts between Orthodox and Enlightened Jews and the Governmental Decision of 26th February, 1814," Studia Rosenthaliana 15 (1981): 20–36.

92. In 1799, David Friedlander sent a letter on behalf of an anonymous group of Jewish families to William Teller, provost of the Berlin Consistory of the Protestant Church, asking that they be admitted to the Christian church without submission to its dogmas. The objective of this "dry baptism" was the acquisition of Prussian citizenship. Teller was unwilling to accept the Jewish heads of families into the church as deists, and, as manifest in the Friedlander letter, the would-be converts did not seek a religious conversion but merely a conversion in name. The letter to Teller and the provost's reply generated extensive literary debate in Berlin. See Meyer, Origins of the Modern Jew, pp. 70–78.

93. From C. L. Paalzow, Die Juden (Berlin, 1799), quoted in Schmidt, "Terms of Emancipation," p. 37.

94. "Briefe bei Gelegenheit der politisch theologischen Aufgabe und des Sendschreibens Judischer Hausvater," Friederich Schleiermacher's Sämtliche Werke, pt. 1: Zur Theologie, 5:1–39, as cited in Meyer, Origins of the Modern Jew, pp. 76–78.

95. The Jews' belief in the Messiah was thought to imply hopes of a political restoration.

96. Johann Gottlieb Fichte, "Beitrag zur Berichtung der Urteile des Publicums ueber die Franzoeische Revolutions," *Sämtliche Werke* (Berlin, 1845), 6: 149–50, quoted in Mendes-Flohr and Reinharz, eds., *Jew in the Modern World*, p. 257.

97. In 1808, Jews had obtained local citizenship. A decision concerning the Jews' participation in government service was deferred to a later time. As the time of renewed battle with Napoleon drew near, even the conservatives in Prussia supported Jewish military service. If Jews did not participate in the war, they believed, the Jews would reap financial benefit while Christians killed one another on the battlefields of Europe (Schmidt, "Terms of Emancipation," p. 33). The text of the Prussian emancipation decree can be found in Ismar Freund, *Die Emanzipation der Juden in Preussen,* vol. 2 (Berlin: Poppelaver, 1912), pp. 455–59.

98. Quoted in Meyer, *Origins of the Modern Jew,* p. 139.

99. On Tabernacles *(Shavuoth)* 1815, Jacobson held a reform service at his home in Berlin. Thereafter, services were held each Saturday morning in his home, at which both Jews and Christians were present. A choir accompanied by organ music also included Christian singers. Prayers were recited in German and Hebrew, and the service was abbreviated by omitting the repetition of the silent devotion and eliminating the *musaf* prayer. The sermon became an important component of Jacobson's service. Eight months after this private service was initiated, it was closed down by order of the king, probably at the instigation of Jewish traditionalists, who considered the reformers religious sectarians. On Jacobson's Berlin service and its closure, see Marcus, "Reform Judaism," pp. 467–68.

100. A related phenomenon was the incorporation of "foreign law" into the proceedings of the Jewish law courts. Thus, for example, a *takkanah* of the Jewish community of Livorno, adopted in 1670, decreed that all disputes arising out of commercial transactions "will be adjudicated in accordance with commercial custom, i.e., by the commercial laws of this city;

we accept them upon ourselves and authorize them as though they had been decided upon by Torah judgment . . . and by their terms will judgments be rendered" (quoted in Shabbatai Toaf, "Maḥaloket Rabbi Ya'acov Sasportas u'Parnessei Livorno," *Sfunot* 9 [1965]: 190–91). The abdication of "Torah law" in commercial affairs by the Livorno community drew the ire of Jacob Sasportas, who polemicized against it (ibid., pp. 169–91).

101. Examples of rabbinic inveighing against resort to Gentile courts abound during the seventeenth and eighteenth centuries. Thus, for example, Rabbi Joseph Staathagen (late seventeenth century) quoted Deut. 17:8–11 as the basis for adjudicating disputes before rabbinic courts, then proceeded to rebuke the Jews of far-flung German communities, who "sometimes refuse to bring their litigation before the sages of the generation [a reference to Deut. 17:8–11] and sometimes *do* bring their dispute before a Jewish court but don't accept the judgment; then they go before the non-Jewish tribunal and even though the judgment, occasionally, is identical to that rendered by the Jewish court, the parties happily accept the verdict. And I say that this matter is included in what we say after the *ashamnu* confessional: 'We have abandoned your commandments and judgments'" (Joseph Staathagen, *Divrei Zikaron* [Amsterdam: Emanuel Athias, 1705], pt. 1, 32b). From a sermon of Jonathan Eybeschutz (mid-eighteenth century), it appears that even synagogue affairs sometimes found their way to non-Jewish courts: "Because of our great sins, pride and self-aggrandizement in the synagogue regarding being summoned to the Torah and receiving other honors during the service . . . [have led] a few times to recourse to non-Jewish courts" (Jonathan Eybeschutz, *Sefer Ya'arot Dvash*, vol. 2 [Salzbach, 1799], p. 17a). Rabbi Raphael ha-Cohen (see n. 45 above) devoted a large part of his final two sermons in Altona, 1799, to the importance of maintaining the Jewish legal system. More than any other element of the erosion of Jewish tradition, he declared, the abandonment of the Jewish legal system was the most serious, for if there was no

resort to Jewish law, there was no Divine Righteousness (based on Isaiah 5:27). See Raphael Cohen, "Zion be-Mishpat," in Eliezer Lazar Katznellenbogen, ed., *Zekher Zadik* (Vilna, 1878). Raphael ha-Cohen's special concern for Jewish courts was related to the expectations of the era in which he lived. If aspects of redemption—such as the rebuilding of the Temple—were imminently possible, it was imperative that the favor of Divine Righteousness be curried.

102. See Elon, *Ha-Mishpat ha-Ivri*, 1:71, esp. n. 18.

103. See the assembly's response to Question 2, above.

104. Jacob Sapir, *Edut Bihosef* (1870), p. 36.

105. Quoted in Max J. Kohler, "Jewish Rights at the Congresses of Vienna and Aix-la-Chapelle," *Publications of the American Jewish Historical Society* 26 (1918): 59–60.

106. Ibid. That the prepositional change was not, at the time of its adoption, generally viewed as effecting a critical change in the meaning of the phrase is evidenced in a letter from Prince Hardenberg to the Senate of Lubeck, dated June 10, 1815—two days after adoption of Article 16—in which he wrote: "Under the terms of Article 16 of the Constitution of the German Confederation, it cannot be doubted that the civil rights of the Jewish inhabitants of the Hanseatic cities are preserved until action by the Diet in the premises, in accordance with the French legislation fixing these rights, and in line with the Prussian legislative policy and the principles of rational toleration" (ibid., p. 63).

Chapter 5

1. See *She'elot u-Teshuvot Hatam Sofer*, Hoshen Mishpat, Resp. 62, 63, 64, 65, 74, 142; Orah Hayim, Resp. 62, 113, 145. In the course of acknowledging the king's right to an inheritance tax under the principle *dina de-malkhuta dina*, Sofer maintained that this was the limit of the king's interest in an inheritance. The balance of the inheritance was to be dealt with in accordance with Jewish legal norms.

Notes to Chapter 5

2. Thus, for example, Bruno Bauer devoted considerable attention to the political-religious distinction in the decisions of the Paris Sanhedrin.

3. From Friedrich Ruhs, *Über die Anspruche der Juden an das deutsche Burgerrecht* (Berlin, 1816), quoted in Jacob Katz, *From Prejudice to Destruction* (Cambridge, Mass.: Harvard University Press, 1980), p. 80.

4. From Jacob Friedrich Fries, *Über die Gafahrdung des Wohlstandes und Charakters der Deutschen durch die Juden* (Heidelberg, 1816), quoted in ibid., p. 82.

5. Trans. in Isaac Barzilay, "The Treatment of the Jewish Religion in the Literature of the Berlin Haskalah," *PAAJR* 24 (1955): 42.

6. On Jacobson's reformist activity, see Chapter 4.

7. Eliezer Lieberman, *Nogah ha-Zedek* (Dessau: K. Schlieder, 1818).

8. *Eleh Divrei ha-Brit* (Altona: Hamburg Beth Din, 1819; rpr. Jerusalem, 1970), p. iv.

9. Quotations are in ibid., pp. 9, 13, and 17; similar statements appear on pp. 22–23, 27, 54, 67, and 91. Sofer's second letter was sent after he had seen a copy of *Nogah ha-Zedek*. In it, he put forward an argument frequently advanced by the traditionalists to government authorities in trying to stamp out reform activities: the God-fearing orthodox were religiously obligated to obey the king and could be trusted to do so, but the reformers were rebels whose oath of loyalty was valueless (*Eleh Divrei ha-Brit*, pp. 41–42). Sofer's third letter carried a retraction from one of the supporters of the Hamburg temple reforms, Aaron Chorin. This retraction, which did not deter Chorin from vigorously supporting reform in the decades ahead, suggested that the assembly of the sages of the generation, authorized to meet by the ruling authority, would be empowered to effect changes in Jewish practice (ibid., p. 98). This view is consistent with the high hopes Chorin had expressed that the Assembly of Notables would "purify" Judaism (see Chapter 4, n. 47). An intermediate position between that of the reformers and the traditionalists on the messianic

issue was articulated by Ziskind Raskow, who while arguing that one who rejects belief in the Messiah rejects, thereby, the words of the prophets, separated the notion of the Messiah from the hope for the restoration to Israel: "Not for the inheritance of our land do we wait nor for temporary, vapid benefits in Israel or outside of it but we look forward to the true happiness of all humankind, collectively and individually and to the fulfillment of the lofty purpose for which God put man upon the face of the earth, that the earth be filled with the knowledge of the Lord" (Ziskind Raskow, *Te'udah be-Yisrael* [Breslau: Leib Zulzbach, 1818], pp. 23–24). On the varying conceptions of the Messiah expressed during the Hamburg temple controversy, 1817–20, see Baruch Mevorach, "Ha-Emunah ba-Mashiah be-Pulmusei ha-Reforma ha-Rishonim," *Zion* 34 (1969): 199–218.

10. In writing of the leading traditionalist rabbis of this period, Heinrich Graetz observed: "These rabbis had not the slightest conception of the new tendency which the times and the Jews had developed. . . . When a serious question or a critical situation arose . . . they brought out their old rusty weapons" (*History of the Jews*, vol. 5 [Philadelphia: Jewish Publication Society, 1956], p. 567). Sofer, for example, argued that, inasmuch as the Sabbath *musaf* service replaced the additional sacrifice that was performed on the Sabbath, the Hamburg reformers were inconsistent in retaining any vestige of this additional Sabbath service because they had no daily service (*Eleh Divrei ha-Brit*, p. 7).

11. The Reform rejoinder to *Eleh Divrei ha-Brit*, Meyer Bresselau, *Herev Nokemet Nekom Brit* (Dessau, 1819), also invoked Jewish legal sources in support of the Hamburg innovations.

12. See, e.g., *She'elot u-Teshuvot Lehem Rav*, 15; *Pahad Yizhak*, section "Zurat Hatan ve-Kallah"; and S. Simonsohn, "Some Disputes on Music in the Synagogue in Pre-Reform Days," *PAAJR* 34 (1966): 99–110.

13. *Eleh Divrei ha-Brit*, p. 55. Moses Sofer did not share this view of Mendelssohn and the traditional *maskilim*. In an

ethical will written for the guidance of his descendants in 1836, he wrote: "May your mind not turn to evil and never engage in corruptible partnership with those fond of innovations, who, as a penalty for our many sins, have strayed from the Almighty and His Law! Do not touch the books of Rabbi Moses [Mendelssohn] from Dessau, and your foot will never slip!" (quoted in Plaut, *Rise of Reform Judaism*, p. 256).

14. On these riots, see Katz, *From Prejudice to Destruction*, pp. 97–104.

15. Immanuel Wolf, "On the Concepts of a Science of Judaism (1822)," trans. Lionel E. Kochan, *LBIY* 2 (1957): 201.

16. Ibid., pp. 203–4.

17. On the history of the Verein, see Meyer, *Origins of the Modern Jew*, pp. 167–82.

18. The immediate aim of Zunz's work was to overcome the Prussian government's prohibition against preaching in the vernacular in the synagogue.

19. Quoted in Samuel Cohen, "Zunz and Reform Judaism," *HUCA* 31 (1960): 256. Independent of the scientific Jewish scholarship in Germany, an eastern European school of Jewish science developed during the same period around Nachman Krochmal (1785–1840). Whereas Zunz argued that scientific examination of Judaism would lead to the elimination of civil disabilities imposed upon German Jews, the Jewish jurist Gabriel Riesser took a different approach in the pursuit of emancipation. Riesser argued: "Religion has its creed; the state its laws. The confession of a creed constitutes a religious affiliation; obedience to laws determines citizenship in a state. . . . There is only one baptism that can initiate one into a nationality, and that is the baptism of blood in the common struggle for a fatherland and for freedom" (quoted in Mendes-Flohr and Reinharz, eds., *Jew in the Modern World*, pp. 130–31). The complete confessionalization of Judaism, described by Riesser in 1831, found expression in the Jewish religious reforms of his generation. On Riesser's role in the struggle for emancipation, see Moshe Rinott, "Gabriel Ries-

ser—Fighter for Jewish Emancipation," *LBIY* 7 (1962):11–38.

20. From Abraham Geiger, *Wissenschaftliche Zeitschrift für Judische Theologie* 4 (1839): 378ff., quoted in Luitpold Wallach, "The Beginnings of the Science of Judaism in the Nineteenth Century," *HJ* 8 (1946): 58–59.

21. Letter of March 19, 1845, in Max Wiener, *Abraham Geiger and Liberal Judaism*, trans. Ernst J. Schlochauer (Philadelphia: Jewish Publication Society, 1962), p. 114.

22. Abraham Geiger, *Wissenschaftliche Zeitschrift für Judische Theologie* 1 (1837): 1–14.

23. An example of the invective and solicitation of government intervention which were part and parcel of the "live" reform-traditionalist confrontations is the Geiger-Tiktin episode in Breslau in 1838–43. Geiger, with the support of reform sympathizers in Breslau, was elected second rabbi to S. A. Tiktin, a traditionalist. A variety of intrigues ensued, aimed at averting the threat of reform. See David Philipson, *The Reform Movement in Judaism* (New York: Ktav Publishing House, 1967), pp. 51–74; Wiener, *Abraham Geiger*, pp. 17–33.

24. Geiger and Hirsch were acquainted, having been students together at the University of Bonn. Fundamental to Hirsch's ideology was the necessity of combining "Torah im derekh erez" (Avot 2:2), which he understood to include secular education and western European culture.

25. Samson Raphael Hirsch, *The Nineteen Letters of Ben Uziel* (New York: Feldheim, 1969). The book is in the form of correspondence between a young, questioning German-Jew and his rabbi friend.

26. Ibid., Letters 2, 3, 4, 7–8, 9, 10, 16. The various categories of commandments and a discussion of their interrelationship are found in Letters 11–14.

27. *Der Orient* (1842), p. 50. Quoted in Landman, *Jewish Law in the Diaspora*, p. 143.

28. The civil-religious distinction yielded ever more to the state in the chain extending from Mendelssohn to the Paris Sanhedrin to the reformers in Germany. Always, however,

Jewish legal authorities had argued that it was Jewish law which defined the category "civil law" for purposes of applying *dina de-malkhuta dina.*

29. Aaron Chorin, *Iggert el Asaf* (Prague: Shallolandi, 1826), p. 39.

30. Holdheim (1806–60) was born in Poland but made his way to Germany during the 1830s, where he became one of the most extreme Jewish religious reformers. From 1847 until his death, he served as rabbi in the reform temple in Berlin.

31. Samuel Holdheim, *Über die Autonomie der Rabbinen und das Princip der Judischen Ehe* (Schwerin: C. Kurschner, 1847), p. 138.

32. Chapter 2, n. 31.

33. Holdheim, *Über die Autonomie der Rabbinen,* pp. 49ff, trans. in Jacob J. Petuchowski, "Abraham Geiger and Samuel Holdheim," *LBIY* 22 (1977): 143.

34. *Protokolle der ersten Rabbiner versammlung* (Brunswick, 1844), p. 29, quoted in Philipson, *Reform Movement in Judaism,* p. 151.

35. Quoted in Philipson, *Reform Movement in Judaism,* p. 278.

36. Ibid., p. 279.

37. On the controversy between Samuel Holdheim and Zachariah Frankel over the nature of marriage in Jewish law, see A. N. Z. Roth, "*Dina de-Malkhuta Dina,*" *ha-Soker* 5 (1937): 114–17.

38. Bauer's *Judenfrage* was published first in the *Deutsche Jahrbucher* in 1842 and then issued in 1843 as a pamphlet. Page references herein are to the English edition, Bruno Bauer, *The Jewish Problem,* trans. Helen Lederer (Cincinnati: Hebrew Union College–Jewish Institute of Religion, 1958). Although Bauer and other Hegelians drew antiemancipatory conclusions with regard to the "Jewish problem," Hegel himself had favored equal rights for the Jews on the basis that denying them such rights would confirm the isolation for which they were reproached. See Shlomo Avineri, "A Note on Hegel's Views on Jewish Emancipation," *JSS* 25 (1963): 145–

51. At the same time that Bruno Bauer was assailing the Jews from the left, Frederick William IV, who yearned to recreate the divine order of the Holy Roman Empire, posed a strong threat from the right. Late in 1841, the king had issued a cabinet order in which he declared: "The efforts of those who seek an improvement in the social situation of the Jews through their individual assimilation into the civil life of the Christian population of the land can never be fruitful and salutary for the mutual relationship of Christians and Jews, since they stand in contradiction to the national type." The king proposed to reorganize the Jews as a minority corporation and to release them from the obligation of military service (Ismar Schorsch, "Ideology and History in the Age of Emancipation," in *The Structure of Jewish History and Other Essays (Graetz)*, ed. Ismar Schorsch [New York: Ktav Publishing House, 1975], pp. 19–20).

39. Bauer, *Jewish Problem*, pp. 32, 112–24.

40. Jer. 29:7.

41. Bauer, *Jewish Problem*, p. 122.

42. Christians must liberate themselves from Christianity in order to become emancipated, but their step to freedom is a much smaller one than the leap the Jew must take. It would be easier for Christians to advance to atheism than for the Jews! See Funkenstein, "Political Theory of Jewish Emancipation," p. 23.

43. References to Marx's *Zur Judenfrage* are cited from the English edition, Karl Marx, *A World without Jews*, trans. Dagobert D. Runes (New York: Philosophical Library, 1950).

44. Ibid., pp. 37–38. Marx further observed: "The God of the Jews has become secularized and is now a worldly God. The bill of exchange is the Jews' real God" (ibid., p. 41).

45. On the participants in the reform conferences of 1844–46, see Steven Lowenstein, "The 1840s and the Creation of the German-Jewish Religious Reform Movement," in *Revolution and Evolution: 1848 in German-Jewish History*, ed. Werner Mosse, Arnold Paucker, and Reinhard Rurup (Tubingen: J. C. B. Mohr, 1981), pp. 264–79.

46. This self-perception of the reformers continued late into the nineteenth century. Thus a compilation of the decisions of past reform conferences, compiled for inclusion in the American Reform Rabbinate's first yearbook, 1890–91, began with a summary of the doctrinal decisions of the Paris Sanhedrin, then proceeded to the reform conferences in Germany, 1844–46.

47. *Protokolle der ersten Rabbinerversammlung,* p. 73, trans. in Philipson, *Reform Movement in Judaism,* p. 150.

48. In Prussia, for example, a Christian was forbidden to marry a non-Christian whose religion did not recognize the validity of the Christian wedding ceremony. In the event of a mixed marriage in compliance with this requirement, children were to be raised in the religion of the father until the age of fourteen (Ismar Schorsch, *Jewish Reactions to German Anti-Semitism, 1870–1914* [New York: Columbia University Press, 1972], p. 9).

49. According to Jewish law, the child's religion is determined by the religion of the mother.

50. *Protokolle,* p. 98.

51. Ibid., p. 41.

52. From the fifth century and into the nineteenth century, Jews testifying in Christian courts were obliged to take a special oath, often embellished with symbolic rituals, invoking God's name and calling various curses upon themselves as a guarantee of truthfulness.

53. The liturgical issues to be resolved were the necessity or advisability of Hebrew language in religious services, the question of the messianic doctrine and whether references to a Messiah had a place in the liturgy, the necessity of repeating the silent devotion and of retaining the additional Sabbath service *(musaf),* means of improving the Sabbath Torah reading, rendering the rites of blowing the *shofar* and waving the *lulav* more aesthetic, and organ music on the Sabbath.

54. *Torat ha-Kena'ot* (Amsterdam: D. Propos, 1845). Separate works were published by Zvi Hirsch Chajes, *Ma'amar Minḥat Kena'ot* (Zolkiew: Markovich and Friedman, 1849);

David Deutsch, *Asof Asifa* (Breslau: H. Salzbach, 1846); Pinḥas Heilpern, *Teshuvot be-Anshei Aven* (Frankfort, 1845); and Solomon Rapoport, *Toḥaḥat Megullah* (Frankfort: Friedrich Bach, 1845).

55. Exod. 23:2.

56. *Torat ha-Kena'ot*, pp. 2, 4b, 8b, 20a, 31b, 9a, 7a. A few of the traditionalist respondents pointed out that beyond the legal problems there were serious social problems involved in intermarriage between Jews and Christians (ibid., pp. 18b, 27b).

57. Ibid., pp. 6b, 7a, 2b, 21a, and 13b.

58. Zachariah Frankel, "Die Rabbinerversammlung zu Braunschweig," *Zeitschrift für Religiose Interessen* 1 (1844): 289–308.

59. A revised edition of the Hamburg reform prayerbook was published in 1841, and the local Orthodox leader, ḥaham Isaac Bernays, immediately proclaimed that anyone who used it would not thereby fulfill the requirements of Jewish worship. Although criticizing Bernay's approach to the problem, Frankel declared that the reformers were in error in undertaking to modify the liturgy drastically. Only *klal yisrael* as a whole could revise Jewish religious usage, in conformity with the spirit of the people (*Der Orient* 3 [1842]: 353–67). On the specific issue of the reformers' omission of prayers for a rebuilt Zion, Frankel wrote: "The idea of an independent Jewish homeland is in itself ennobling and full of vitality. There is nothing wrong in the aspiration to re-establish our nationality in a corner of the globe, associated with our most sacred memories, where it could again stride forward freely, and gain the respect of the nations, which sad experience teaches us is extended only to those who possess worldly power. In this hope, there is no inkling of hate or disparagement of our present Fatherland; nor should it arouse a suspicion that we regard ourselves as aliens in the Fatherland and that we desire to flee from it. . . . This merely proves that despite millennia of suffering and oppression, we have not yet despaired and we are still in a position to grasp the idea of independence and re-

generation. In any case, this is a far loftier concept than the constant subservient accommodation of our people to external conditions, an attempt which frequently culminates in a vapid, superficial cosmopolitanism" (ibid., p. 363, quoted in David Rudavsky, "The Historical School of Zachariah Frankel," *JSS* 5 [1963]: 233).

60. To increase his understanding of the *volksgeist* of the Jewish people, Frankel devoted considerable study to the history of Jewish law. One of Frankel's early works, *The Jewish Oath in Theological and Historical Context* (1840), helped to abolish the oath *more Judaica* in several German states.

61. That Frankfort was the site of the conference was not by arbitrary decision. Since 1843, a Frankfort Society of the Friends of Reform had been active in that city. Its declaration of principles proclaimed: "(1) We recognize the possibility of unlimited development in the Mosaic religion. (2) The collection of controversies, dissertations, and prescriptions commonly designated by the name Talmud possesses for us no authority either from the dogmatic or practical standpoint. (3) A Messiah who is to lead back the Israelites to the land of Palestine is neither expected nor desired by us; we know no fatherland except that to which we belong by birth or citizenship" (quoted in Philipson, *Reform Movement in Judaism*, p. 133).

62. The conference held that the retention of Hebrew in the liturgy was neither objectively nor subjectively necessary but was merely advisable. The importance of Hebrew to Jewish life was also championed by Moses Israel Chazan, who, as an emissary of Palestine Jewry to England in 1845, wrote in a tract to English Jewry: "Above all, let me remind you that it is incumbent upon every Israelite, male and female, to have his children instructed in the language of your nation, viz. the sacred tongue. The social intercourse of a people consists in three things: 1. Joining together in eating and drinking; 2. Intermarrying; 3. Speaking the same language. As to the first and second, we have no cause to complain; but as to the third, we are grieved to see that we are not closely united in lan-

guage. What nation is there on earth who have themselves neglected their language as, alas! we have neglected ours?" (Israel Moshe Chazan, *Words of Peace and Truth* [London: S. Meldola, 1845], p. 13). The same author wrote a treatise on inheritance law in 1851, in which he emphasized the inapplicability of *dina de-malkhuta dina* to matters of inheritance: "Of what bearing is *dina de-malkhuta* on the Biblical law of inheritance? . . . Go and inquire in the rabbinical houses of study in all parts of the globe and you will find clearly, by the lights of the sun, that the Jews who seek an inheritance against the law of Moses are adjudged Sadduccean heretics uprooters of the Torah, notorious thieves; and if you will investigate them you will discover that they transgress otherwise" (Israel Moshe Chazan, *Nahala le-Yisrael* [Vienna: Delatorre, 1851], pp. 46–47). Evidently, as in the case of the decline of Hebrew study, recourse to "foreign law" in inheritance matters had become widespread. Although the phrase "positive historical" Judaism is somewhat vague, Frankel apparently used the word "positive" to represent the core or preservative values and observances of Judaism, of which Hebrew was one, and "historical" to refer to the development of these traditions over time.

63. As the Frankfort Conference devoted most of its attention to liturgical issues, so did the Breslau Conference focus on the question of Sabbath observance.

64. Heilpern, *Teshuvot be-Anshei Aven*, p. 71.

65. *Allgemeine Zeitung des Judentums* 12 (1848): 210, quoted in Reinhard Rurup, "The European Revolutions of 1848 and Jewish Emancipation," in *Revolution and Evolution*, ed. Mosse, Paucker, and Rurup, p. 49.

66. Of Holdheim, Graetz, his contemporary, wrote: "Had he lived in the time of the Maccabbees, Holdheim would have joined the renegade Menelaus in urging the Jews to worship the Greek Zeus, because the state, which was then called Antiochus Epiphanes, had so commanded" (Graetz, *History of the Jews*, 5: 681).

67. The Breslau Seminary, established in 1854, was headed

197

by Zachariah Frankel and trained rabbis and teachers in the positive-historical approach.

68. *Der Orient* 9 (1848): 437, quoted in Rurup, "European Revolutions," p. 50.

Glossary

Agunah. Literally, "tied"; a married woman who is separated from her husband but who cannot remarry.

Aḥaronim. Literally, "later ones"; refers to rabbinic scholars from the time of the *Shulkhan Arukh* (code of Jewish law compiled in the sixteenth century) to the emancipation, two centuries later.

Amoraim. Literally, "speakers"; Talmudic sages of the third through the fifth centuries.

Apikoros. Agnostic.

Arkha'ot shel goyim. Gentile judicial tribunals.

Arus(a). One who is affianced.

Bet din. Jewish law court.

Dina de-malkhuta dina. "The law of the kingdom is law."

Erusin. Formal act of betrothal leading to change in personal status of the affianced from bachelorhood toward marriage; also called *Kiddushin*.

Eruv. An encirclement, either by walls or wires, meeting certain specifications, within which carrying on the Sabbath is permissible.

Exilarch. "Head of the Exile"; political head of the Babylonian Jewish community.

Gemara. Closing (and most voluminous) section of the Talmud; record of oral discussion of the *mishnah* edited early in the sixth century.

Geonim. Heads of the Babylonian academies from the sixth century until early in the eleventh century.

Get. Jewish divorce document.

Gezelah de-malkhuta. Literally, "robbery of the kingdom"; a seizure of property, by the kingdom, deemed illegal by Jewish law.

Gillui arayot. Biblically prohibited marriages.

Halakhah. Jewish law.

Ḥaliza. Ceremony whereby a widowed woman becomes released from a levirate tie (i.e., prospective marriage to the brother of the deceased husband if he had died without offspring).

Haskalah. "Enlightenment."

Hefker bet din hefker. Authority of Jewish legal scholars to enact even such ordinances as may involve uprooting a law of the Torah.

Ḥerem. Excommunication.

Ḥerem de-Rabbenu Gershom. Prohibition of polygamy by the early eleventh-century German Jewish scholar Rabbenu Gershom ben Judah, on pain of excommunication.

Hora'at sha'ah. Emergency power assumed by rabbis in criminal matters. Exigency jurisdiction.

Hurmena de-malka. Royal regulations.

Issur ve-hetter. Religious (ritual) prohibitions and observances.

Kashrut. Jewish dietary laws.

Kehillah. Jewish community.

Ketubbah. Jewish marriage document recording a husband's obligations toward his wife.

Kiddushin. Act performed between a man and a woman which changes personal status from bachelorhood but does not fully effectuate marriage. Also called *erusin*.

Malshin. "Slanderer."

Mamona. Commercial law.

Maskil. "Enlightened" individual.

Mesirah. Turning over an alleged criminal to government authorities for prosecution.

Mishnah. Compilation of oral law early in the third century; constitutes the first section of the Talmud.

Nissu'in. Marriage, before two competent witnesses, "according to the law of Moses and Israel."

Parnassim. Lay leaders of the *kehillot* (Jewish communities).

Piyyutim. Liturgical poems.

Rishonim. Literally, "early ones"; refers to rabbinic scholars from the eleventh through the fifteenth centuries.

Semikhah. Rabbinic ordination.

Shulkhan Arukh. Jewish code of law.

Syag la-Torah. Literally, "fence around the law"; rabbinic enactments expanding legal strictures, designed to assure observance of the principal laws.

Takkanah. Rabbinic ordinance.

Tanaim. Scholars of the second century B.C.E. through the second century C.E. whose teachings are quoted in the Mishnah.

General Bibliography

Abrahams, Israel. *Jewish Life in the Middle Ages*. London: E. Goldston, Ltd., 1932.

Abramsky, Chimen. "The Crisis of Authority within European Jewry in the Eighteenth Century." In *Studies in Jewish Religious and Intellectual History*, edited by Siegfried Stein and Raphael Loewe, pp. 13–38. University, Ala.: University of Alabama Press, 1979.

"Afk'inhu Rabanan le-Kiddushin Minei." *Encyclopedia Talmudit*, 2:137–40. Jerusalem, 1949.

Agus, Irving. *Rabbi Meir of Rothenburg*. Vol. 1. Philadelphia: Dropsie College, 1947.

———. *Teshuvot Ba'alei ha-Tosafot*. New York: Talpiyot, 1954.

Albeck, Shalom. "Dina De-Malkhuta Dina be-Kehillot Sefarad." In *Abraham Weiss Jubilee Volume*, pp. 109–16. New York: Shulsinger Bros., 1964.

Altmann, Alexander. *Moses Mendelssohn*. University, Ala.: University of Alabama Press, 1973.

Amram, D. W. *The Jewish Law of Divorce According to the Bible and the Talmud*. Philadelphia: Press of E. Stern and Co., 1896.

Anchel, Robert. *Les Juifs de France*. Paris: J. B. Janin, 1946.

General Bibliography

Anderson, Matthew S. *Europe in the Eighteenth Century, 1713–1783.* London: Oxford University Press, 1976.

Asaf, Simha. *Teshuvot ha-Geonim.* Jerusalem: Hebrew University, ha-Madpis, 1942.

Avineri, Shlomo. "A Note on Hegel's Views on Jewish Emancipation." *JSS* 25 (1963): 145–51.

Azulai, Haim Joseph David. *Sefer Ma'agal Tov ha-Shalem.* Jerusalem: Mekize Nirdamim, 1934.

Bachi, Ricard. "Osef Hadash Shel Te'udot Al Yehudei Italia Biymei Napoleon." *Zion* 7 (1941): 51–54.

Baer, Yizhak. "Ha-Yesodot ve-ha-Hathalot Shel Irgun ha-Kehillah ha-Yehudit Biymei ha-Beina'im." *Zion* 15 (1950): 1–41.

Baron, Salo W. *The Jewish Community.* Vols. 1, 2, and 3. Philadelphia: Jewish Publication Society, 1942.

_____. "The Revolution of 1848 and Jewish Scholarship." *PAAJR* 18 (1948–49): 1–66; 20 (1951): 1–100.

_____. *A Social and Religious History of the Jews.* Vols. 3, 5, 9. Philadelphia: Jewish Publication Society, 1957.

Barzilay, Isaac. "The Background of the Berlin Haskalah." In *Essays in Honor of Salo W. Baron,* edited by Joseph L. Blau, pp. 183–97. New York: Columbia University Press, 1959.

_____. "The Ideology of the Berlin Haskalah." *PAAJR* 25 (1956): 1–37.

_____. "Moses Mendelssohn." *JQR* 52 (1961): 69–93, 175–86.

_____. *SHIR and His Contemporaries.* Ramat Gan: Massada, 1969.

_____. "The Treatment of the Jewish Religion in the Literature of the Berlin Haskalah." *PAAJR* 24 (1955): 39–68.

Bauer, Bruno. *The Jewish Problem.* Translated by Helen Lederer. Cincinnati: Hebrew Union College–Jewish Institute of Religion, 1958.

Baumgarten, Albert. "Justinian and the Jews." In *Joseph H. Lookstein Memorial Volume,* edited by Leo Landman, pp. 37–44. New York: Ktav Publishing House, 1980.

Beloff, Max. *The Age of Absolutism, 1660–1815.* New York: Hutchinson's University Library, 1954.

General Bibliography

Ben-Dov, S. "Dina de-Malkhuta Dina." *Talpiyot* 7 (1961–65): 395–405; 8:79–84; 9:230–37.

Ben-Sasson, H. H., ed. *A History of the Jewish People.* Cambridge, Mass.: Harvard University Press, 1976.

Bernfeld, Simon. *Ha-Reformation ha-Datit be-Yisrael.* Warsaw: Ahiasaf, 1900.

Blau, Joseph L. *Modern Varieties of Judaism.* New York: Columbia University Press, 1966.

Blidstein, Gerald J. "A Note on the Function of 'The Law of the Kingdom Is Law' in the Medieval Jewish Community." *JJS* 15 (1973): 213–19.

Bloom, Solomon F. "Karl Marx and the Jews." *JSS* 4 (1942): 3–16.

Blumenkranz, Bernhard, ed. *Le Grand Sanhedrin de Napoleon.* Toulouse: E. Privat, 1979.

Bresselau, Meyer. *Herev Nokemet Nekom Brit.* Dessau, 1819.

Carsten, Francis L. "The Court Jews: A Prelude to Emancipation." *LBIY* 3 (1958): 140–56.

Chajes, Zvi Hirsch. *Ma'amar Minhat Kena'ot.* Zolkiew: Markovich and Friedman, 1849.

Chazzan, Israel Moshe. *Nahala le-Yisrael.* Vienna: Delatorre, 1851.

———. *Words of Peace and Truth.* London: S. Meldola, 1845.

Chazan, Robert, ed. *Church, State and Jew in the Middle Ages.* New York: Behrman House, 1980.

Chorin, Aaron. *Iggeret el Asaf.* Prague: Shallolandi, 1826.

———. "Letter to the Assembly of Notables." Central Archives for the History of the Jewish People, HM 24 (microfilm of Themanlys Archives).

Cohen, Boaz. "Civil Marriage" (Appendix). *Proceedings of the Rabbinical Assembly of America* 6 (1939): 141–45.

Cohen, Daniel Y. "Irgunei Bnei ha-Medina be-Ashkenaz be-Meiot ha-17-18." Ph.D. dissertation, Hebrew University, 1967.

Cohen, Jeremy. *The Friars and the Jew.* Ithaca: Cornell University Press, 1982.

Cohen, Samuel. "Zunz and Reform Judaism." *HUCA* 36 (1960): 251–76.

Daiches, Samuel. "Divorce in Jewish Law." *Studies in Jewish Jurisprudence* 2 (1974): 215–24.

Davis, Moshe. "Mixed Marriage in Western Jewry: Historical Background to the Jewish Response." *JSS* 10 (1968): 177–220.

Décisions doctrinales du Grand Sanhedrin. Paris: Sétier fils, 1812.

Deutsch, David. *Asof Asifa.* Breslau: H. Salzbach, 1846.

"Dina de-Malkhuta Dina." *Encyclopedia Talmudit,* 7:295–308. Jerusalem, 1949.

Dohm, Christian Wilhelm von. *Concerning the Amelioration of the Civil Status of the Jews.* Translated by Helen Lederer. Cincinnati: Hebrew Union College–Jewish Institute of Religion, 1957.

Dubnow, Simon. *History of the Jews.* Translated by Moshe Spiegel. Vol. 4. South Brunswick, N.J.: T. Yoseloff, 1971.

Duker, Abraham G., ed. *Emancipation and Counter-Emancipation.* New York: Ktav Publishing House, 1974.

Eleh Divrei ha-Brit. Altona: Hamburg Beth Din, 1819. Rpr. Jerusalem, 1970.

Ellinsohn, Eliakim. "Dina de-Malkhuta Dina u-Gedarov." *Sinai* 70 (1972): 242–44.

Ellinson, Getsel. "Civil Marriage in Israel: Halakhic and Social Implications." *Tradition* 13 (1972): 242–34.

Elon, Menachem. *Ha-Mishpat ha-Ivri.* 2 vols. Jerusalem: Magnes Press, 1977.

_____. *The Principles of Jewish Law.* Jerusalem: Keter Publishing House, 1975.

_____. "Taxation." *Encyclopedia Judaica,* 15:837–72. Jerusalem, 1971.

Epstein, Louis M. "The Institution of Concubinage among the Jews." *PAAJR* 6 (1934–35): 153–88.

Ettinger, Shmuel. "The Beginnings of the Change in the Attitude of European Society towards the Jew." In *Scripta Hierosolymitana,* 7: 193–219. Jerusalem: Magnes Press, 1961.

_____. "The Modern Period." In *A History of the Jewish Peo-*

ple, edited by H. H. Ben-Sasson. Cambridge, Mass.: Harvard University Press, 1976.

Eybeschutz, Jonathan. *Sefer Ya'arot Dvash.* Vol. 2. Salzbach, 1799.

"Eyn Adam Oseh Be'iylato Be'iylat Znut." *Encyclopedia Talmudit*, 1:257–61. Jerusalem: Mosad ha-Rav Kook, 1978.

Falk, Ze'ev W. *Jewish Matrimonial Law in the Middle Ages.* London: Oxford University Press, 1966.

Finkelstein, Louis. *Jewish Self-Government in the Middle Ages.* New York: P. Feldheim, 1964.

Fleming, James, Jr., and Hazard, Geoffrey, C., Jr. *Civil Procedure.* 2d ed. Boston: Little, Brown, 1977.

Ford, Franklin. *Europe, 1780–1830.* London: Harlow, Longmans, 1970.

Frankel, Zachariah. "Die Rabbinerversammlung zu Braunschweig." *Zeitschrift für Religiose Interessen* 1 (1844): 289–308.

Freimann, Avraham. *Seder Kiddushin ve-Nissu'in Aharei Hatimat ha-Talmud.* Jerusalem: Mosad ha-Rav Kook, 1945.

Freund, Ismar. *Die Emanzipation der Juden in Preussen.* Vol. 2. Berlin: Poppelaver, 1912.

Friedlander, David. *Lesebuch für Judische Kinder.* Berlin: Soncino, 1927.

Funkenstein, Amos. "Changes in the Patterns of Christian Anti-Jewish Polemics in the 12th Century." *Zion* 33 (1968): 125–44.

———. "The Political Theory of Jewish Emancipation from Mendelssohn to Herzl." *Jahrbuch des Instituts für Deutsche Geschichte* 3 (1980): 13–28.

———. "Review of Alexander Altmann's *Moses Mendelssohn*." *AJS Newsletter*, June 1974, 14–16.

Geiger, Abraham. *Wissenschaftliche Zeitschrift für Judische Theologie* 1 (1837): 1–14.

Gelber, N. M. "Napoleon ve-Erez Yisrael." In *Sefer Dinabourg*, edited by Yitzhak Baer, pp. 263–88. Jerusalem: Kiryat Sefer, 1948.

———. "La police autrichienne et le Sanhedrin de Napoleon." *REJ* 83 (1927): 1–21, 113–45.

Glueckel of Hameln. *Memoirs of Glueckel of Hameln.* Translated by Marvin Lowenthal. New York: Harper and Bros., 1932.

Graetz, Heinrich. *History of the Jews.* Vol. 5. Philadelphia: Jewish Publication Society, 1956.

Graupe, Heinz M. *The Rise of Modern Judaism: An Intellectual History of German Jewry, 1650–1942.* New York: R. E. Krieger Publishing Co., 1979.

Greene, Wallace. "Extra-legal Juridical Prerogatives." *Journal for the Study of Judaism* 7 (1976): 152–76.

Grégoire, Henri. *An Essay on the Physical, Moral and Political Regeneration of the Jews.* London: C. Forster, 1791.

Gulak, Asher. *Yesodei ha-Mishpat ha-Ivri: Torat ha-Mishpaḥa ve-ha-Yerusha.* Vol. 3. Berlin: Dvir, 1922.

Halphen, A. E. *Recueil des lois concernant les Israelites dupuis la Revolution.* Paris, 1851.

Hazard, Paul. *The European Mind, 1680–1715.* Cleveland: World Publishing Co., 1969.

Heilpern, Pinḥas. *Teshuvot be-Anshei Aven.* Frankfort, 1845.

Herold, J. Christopher. *The Mind of Napoleon.* New York: Columbia University Press, 1955.

Hertzberg, Arthur. *The French Enlightenment and the Jews.* New York: Columbia University Press, 1968.

Herzog, Isaac. "Din ha-Melekh ve-Din ha-Torah." *Talpiyot* 7 (1965): 4–32.

———. *The Main Institutions of Jewish Law.* Vol. 1. London: Soncino Press, 1965.

Hirsch, Samson Raphael. *The Nineteen Letters of Ben Uziel.* New York: Feldheim, 1969.

Hoenig, Sidney B. *The Great Sanhedrin.* New York: Bloch Publishing Co., 1953.

Holdheim, Samuel. *Über die Autonomie der Rabbinen und das Princip der Judischen Ehe.* Schwerin: C. Kurschner, 1847.

Holtman, Robert B. *The Napoleonic Revolution.* Philadelphia: Lippincott, 1967.

"Hora'at Sha'ah." *Encyclopedia Talmudit,* 8:521–27. Jerusalem, 1957.

General Bibliography

Josephus Flavius. *Antiquities of the Jews*. Translated by William Whiston. New York: W. Borradaile, 1824.

Kahana, Koppel. *The Theory of Marriage in Jewish Law*. Leiden: E. J. Brill, 1966.

Kahana, Y. Z. "Sherut ha-Zava be-Sifrut ha-Teshuvot." *Sinai* 23 (1948): 129–61.

Katz, Jacob. *Emancipation and Assimilation*. Farnborough: Gregg International Publishers, 1972.

―――. *Exclusiveness and Tolerance*. New York: Schocken, 1962.

―――. *From Prejudice to Destruction*. Cambridge, Mass.: Harvard University Press, 1980.

―――. "Kavim le-Bibliographia shel ha-Hatam Sofer." In *Studies in Mysticism and Religion Presented to Gershom Scholem*, edited by Ephraim Urbach, Chaim Werblowsky, and Zvi Werblowsky. Jerusalem: Magnes Press, 1967.

―――. "Mahaloket ha-Semikhah Bein Rabbi Ya'akov Berab ve-ha-Ralbah." *Zion* 16 (1951): 28–45.

―――. *Out of the Ghetto: The Social Background of Jewish Emancipation, 1770–1871*. New York: Schocken, 1978.

―――. "Shlosha Mishpatim Apologeti'im be-Gilguleihem." *Zion* 23–24 (1958–59): 174–93.

―――. *Tradition and Crisis*. New York: Free Press of Glencoe, 1961.

Katznellenbogen, Eliezer Lazar, ed. *Zekher Zadik*. Vilna, 1878.

Kern, Fritz. *Kingship and Law in the Middle Ages*. Translated by S. B. Chrimes. Oxford: B. Blackwell, 1939.

Kisch, Guido. "Relations between Jewish and Christian Courts in the Middle Ages." In *Louis Ginzberg Jubilee Volume*. New York: American Academy for Jewish Research, 1945.

Kober, Adolph. "The French Revolution and the Jews in Germany." *JSS* 7 (1945): 291–322.

Kobler, Franz. *Napoleon and the Jews*. New York: Schocken, 1975.

Kohler, Kaufman. "Harmonization of Marriage and Divorce Laws." *CCARY* 25 (1915): 335–78.

Kohler, Max J. "Jewish Rights at the Congresses of Vienna and Aix-la-Chapelle." *Publications of the American Jewish Historical Society* 26 (1918): 33–125.

Landau, Ezekiel. *Sefer Ḥukei ha-Ishut al Pi Dat Moshe ve-ha-Talmud*. Translated by Z. Scheirblum. Munkacz: Cohen and Fried, 1902.

Landman, Leo. *Jewish Law in the Diaspora: Confrontation and Accommodation*. Philadelphia: Dropsie College, 1968.

Lecestre, Leon. *Lettres inédites de Napoleon I.* Vol. 1. Paris, 1897.

Levi, Israel. "Napoleon I et la reunion du Grand Sanhedrin." *REJ* 28 (1894): 265–80.

Levin, B. M., ed. *Oẓar ha-Geonim*. Vol. 8. Ketubbot. Jerusalem: Mosad ha-Rav Kook, 1938.

Liber, Maurice. "Les Juifs et la convocation des Etats Généraux." *REJ* 63 (1912): 185–210; 64 (1912): 89–109, 144–77; 65 (1913): 161–212.

Lieberman, Eliezer. *Nogah ha-Ẓedek*. Dessau: K. Schlieder, 1818.

Loeb, Isidore. "Les Juifs à Strasbourg depuis 1349 jusqu'a la Révolution." *Annuaire de la Société des Etudes Juives* 2 (1883): 139–98.

Lowenstein, Steven. "The 1840s and the Creation of the German-Jewish Religious Reform Movement." In *Revolution and Evolution: 1848 in German Jewish History*, edited by Werner Mosse, Arnold Paucker, and Reinhard Rurup. Tubingen: J. C. B. Mohr, 1981.

Lowenthal, Marvin. *The Jews of Germany*. Philadelphia: Jewish Publication Society, 1936.

Luzatto, Simḥa. *Ma'amar al Yehudei Veneẓia*. Jerusalem: Mosad Bialik, 1950.

Mahler, Raphael. *A History of Modern Jewry, 1780–1815*. New York: Schocken, 1971.

————, ed. *Jewish Emancipation: A Selection of Documents*. New York: American Jewish Committee, 1941.

Malino, Frances. *The Sephardic Jews of Bordeaux*. University, Ala.: University of Alabama Press, 1978.

Mann, Jacob. "The Responsa of the Babylonian Geonim as a Source of Jewish History." *JQR* 10 (1919): 121–51.

Mantel, Hugo. *Studies in the History of the Sanhedrin.* Cambridge, Mass.: Harvard University Press, 1961.

Marcus, Jacob R. *The Jew in the Medieval World.* Cincinnati: Union of American Hebrew Congregations, 1938.

––––––. "Reform Judaism and the Laity: Israel Jacobson." *CCARY* 38 (1928): 386–498.

Marx, Karl. *A World without Jews.* Translated by Dagobert D. Runes. New York: Philosophical Library, 1950.

Maslin, Simeon J. *Selected Documents of Napoleonic Jewry.* Cincinnati: Hebrew Union College–Jewish Institute of Religion, 1957.

Mazuz, Issachar M. "Nissu'in Ezrahi'im ve-Toza'oteihem." *Shenaton ha-Mishpat ha-Ivri* 3–4 (1976–77): 233–70.

Mendelssohn, Moses. *Gesammelte Schriften,* Vol. 5. Leipzig: Brockhaus, 1844; Vol. 19. Stuttgart: F. Frommann, 1974.

––––––. *Jerusalem and Other Jewish Writings.* Translated by A. Jospe. New York: Schocken, 1969.

Mendes-Flohr, Paul, and Jehuda Reinharz, eds. *The Jew in the Modern World: A Documentary History.* New York: Oxford University Press, 1980.

Mevorach, Baruch. "Ha-Emunah ba-Mashiah be-Pulmusei ha-Reforma ha-Rishonim." *Zion* 34 (1969): 189–218.

––––––. *Napoleon u-Tekufato.* Jerusalem: Mosad Bialik, 1968.

––––––. *Ha-Yehudim Tahat Shilton Napoleon.* Internal Publication of the Hebrew University. Jerusalem, 1970.

Meyer, Michael. "Jewish Religious Reform and Wissenschaft des Judenthums." *LBIY* 16 (1971): 19–41.

––––––. *The Origins of the Modern Jew.* Detroit: Wayne State University Press, 1967.

––––––. "Where Does the Modern Period of Jewish History Begin?" *Judaism* 24 (1975): 329–38.

Michman, J. "The Conflicts between Orthodox and Enlightened Jews and the Governmental Decision of 26th February, 1814." *Studia Rosenthaliana* 15 (1981): 20–36.

General Bibliography

Mielziner, Moses. *The Jewish Law of Marriage and Divorce.* New York: Bloch Publishing Co., 1901.

"Miscellen" [regarding David Sinzheim]. *Sulamith* 1 (1806): 183–84.

Napoleon. *Correspondance.* Paris: H. Plon, 1863.

Necheles, Ruth F. "The Abbé Grégoire and the Jews." *JSS* 33 (1971): 120–40.

Neuman, Abraham A. *The Jews in Spain.* Vol. 1. Philadelphia: Jewish Publication Society, 1942.

Neusner, Jacob. *A History of the Jews in Babylonia.* Vol. 2. Leiden: E. J. Brill, 1966.

Parkes, James. *The Conflict of Church and Synagogue.* London: Soncino Press, 1934.

Pelli, Moshe. "Milḥemet ha-Rav Aharon Chorin Be'ad Reforma Datit ba-Yahadut." *HUCA* 39 (1968): 63–79.

———. *Naphtali Herz Wessely's Attitude toward the Jewish Religion as a Mirror of a Generation in Transition.* Beersheva: University of the Negev, 1971.

Petuchowski, Jacob J. "Abraham Geiger and Samuel Holdheim." *LBIY* 22 (1977): 139–59.

Philipson, David. *The Reform Movement in Judaism.* New York: Ktav Publishing House, 1967.

Philippson, Ludwig. *The Development of the Religious Idea in Judaism, Christianity and Mohomedanism.* Translated by A. M. Goldsmid. London: Longman, Brown, Green and Longmans, 1855.

Plaut, W. Gunther. *The Rise of Reform Judaism.* New York: World Union for Progressive Judaism, 1969.

Posener, S. "The Social Life of the Jewish Communities in France in the Eighteenth Century." *JSS* 7 (1945): 195–232.

Protokolle der ersten Rabbiner versammlung. Brunswick, 1844.

Quint, Emanuel B., and Neil S. Hecht. *Jewish Jurisprudence.* Vol. 1. New York: Harwood Academic Publishers, 1980.

Rakefet-Rothkoff, Aaron. "Dina De-Malkhuta Dina—The Law of the Land in Halakhic Perspective." *Tradition* 13 (1972): 5–23.

Rakover, Nahum. "Dina de-Malkhuta Dina u-Gedarov." *Sinai* 69 (1971): 246–57.

_____. *Ozar ha-Mishpat*. Jerusalem: Harry Fishel Institute, 1975.

Raphael, Shilo. "Nissu'in Ezrahi'im." *Torah she-Be'al Peh* 12 (1970) 108–14.

Rapoport, Solomon. *Tohahat Megullah*. Frankfort: Jakob Friedrich Bach, 1845.

Raskow, Ziskind. *Te'udah be'Yisrael*. Breslau: Leib Zulzbach, 1818.

Rinott, Moshe. "Gabriel Riesser—Fighter for Jewish Emancipation." *LBIY* 7 (1962): 11–38.

Rodner, Abraham A. *Mishpetei Ishut*. Jerusalem: ha-Poel ha-Mizrahi, 1948.

Rotenstreich, Nathan. "For and against Emancipation: The Bruno Bauer Controversy." *LBIY* 4 (1959): 3–36.

_____. "Mendelssohn's Political Philosophy." *LBIY* 11 (1966): 28–41.

Roth, A.N.Z. "Bein Yehudim le-Goyim be-Italia be-Reishit ha-Meah ha-19." In *Hagut Ivrit be-Europa*, edited by Menahem Zohari and Arie Tartakover, pp. 360–75. Tel-Aviv: Yavneh, 1969.

_____. "Dina de-Malkhuta Dina." *ha-Soker* 5 (1937): 110–25.

Roth, Cecil. *The History of the Jews of Italy*. Philadelphia: Jewish Publication Society, 1946.

Rubenstein, Shmuel. "Nissuin Ezrahi'im ba-Halakha." *Torah she-Be'al Peh* 3 (1961): 49–56.

Rudavsky, David. "The Historical School of Zacharia Frankel." *JJS* 5 (1963): 224–44.

Rurup, Reinhard. "The European Revolutions of 1848 and Jewish Emancipation." In *Revolution and Evolution: 1848 in German Jewish History*, edited by Werner Mosse, Arnold Paucker, and Reinhard Rurup, pp. 1–53. Tubingen: J.C.B. Mohr, 1981.

Samet, Moshe S. "Halakha ve-Reforma." Ph.D. dissertation, Hebrew University, 1967.

————. "Ma-avako shel Ḥatam Sofer ba-Ḥadshanim." In *Yehudei Hungaria*, edited by Eliahu Gunda, Yosef Cohen, and Yehuda Martin, pp. 92–103. Tel Aviv: Lahav Press, 1980.

Sapir, Jacob. *Edut Bihosef.* 1870.

Schachter, Jacob. *"Dina de-Malkhuta Dina—A Review."* *Diné Israel* 7 (1977): 77–95.

Schereschewsky, Ben-Zion. "Divorce." *EJ*, 6:122–37. Jerusalem: Keter, 1971.

————. "Marriage." *EJ*, 11:1025–51. Jerusalem: Keter, 1971.

————. "Marriage, Prohibited." *EJ*, 11:1051–54. Jerusalem: Keter, 1971.

Schmidt, H. D. "The Terms of Emancipation, 1781–1812." *LBIY* 1 (1956): 28–47.

Schöffer, I. "The Jews of the Netherlands: The Position of a Minority through Three Centuries." *Studia Rosenthaliana* 15 (1981): 85–100.

Schorsch, Ismar. "Ideology and History in the Age of Emancipation." In *The Structure of Jewish History and Other Essays (Graetz)*, edited by Ismar Schorsch, pp. 1–62. New York: Ktav Publishing House, 1975.

————. *Jewish Reactions to German Anti-Semitism, 1870–1914.* New York: Columbia University Press, 1972.

Schreiber, Emanuel. *Reformed Judaism and Its Pioneers.* Spokane, 1892.

Schwarzfuchs, Simon. "Correspondance du Consistoire Central." *Michael* 1 (1972): 109–62.

————. *Napoleon, the Jews and the Sanhedrin.* London: Routledge & Kegan Paul, 1979.

————. *Le registre des deliberations de la nation Juive Portugaise de Bordeaux.* Paris: Fundaçao Colouste Gulbienkian Centra Cultural Portugues, 1981.

Sharf, Andrew. *Byzantine Jewry.* London: Schocken, 1971.

Shilo, Shmuel. "Dina De-Malkhuta Dina." *EJ*, 6:51–55. Jerusalem: Hebrew University, 1971.

————. *Dina De-Malkhuta Dina.* Jerusalem: Hebrew University, 1974.

_____. "Wills." *EJ*, 16:519–30. Jerusalem: Keter, 1971.

Shohet, Azriel. *Im Hilufei Tekufot: Reishit ha-Haskalah be-Yahadut Germania.* Jerusalem: Mosad Bialik, 1960.

Shohet, David M. *The Jewish Court in the Middle Ages.* New York: Commonday, Roth Co., 1931.

Shulim, Joseph. "Napoleon I as the Jewish Messiah: Some Contemporary Conceptions in Virginia." *JSS* 7 (1945): 175–280.

Sierra, Yosef. "Behinot Shonot shel Da'at ha-Kahal ha-Yehudit be-Italia al ha-Sanhedrin shel Napoleon." In *Hagut Ivrit be-Europa,* edited by Menahem Zohari and Arie Tartakover, pp. 350–60. Tel Aviv: Yavneh, 1969.

Silberg, Moshe. *Talmudic Law and the Modern State.* New York: Burning Bush Press, 1973.

Simonsohn, S. "Some Disputes on Music in the Synagogue in Pre-Reform Days." *PAAJR* 34 (1966): 99–110.

Sinzheim, David. *Minhat Ani.* Jerusalem: Machon Yerushalayim, 1974.

_____. *Yad David.* Jerusalem: Machon Yerushalayim, 1976.

Slama, Guy. "Le mariage en Israel: Une source de conflict entre autorités civile et religieuse." Ph.D. dissertation, Université de Nice, 1976.

Spinoza, Baruch. *Tractatus Theologica-Politicus.* Translated by R.H.M. Elwes. London: Bohn's Philosophical Library, 1883.

Staathagen, Joseph. *Divrei Zikaron.* Amsterdam: Emanuel Athias, 1705.

Steinhardt, Mendel. *Divrei Iggeret.* Roedelheim: Wolf Heidenheim, 1812.

Stern-Taeubler, Selma. *The Court Jew.* Philadelphia: Jewish Publication Society, 1950.

_____. "The First Generation of Emancipated Jews." *LBIY* 15 (1970): 3–40.

_____. "The Jew in the Transition from Ghetto to Emancipation." *HJ* 2 (1940): 102–19.

_____. "The Jews in the Economic Policy of Frederick the Great." *JSS* 11 (1949): 124–52.

————. *Der Preussische Staat und die Juden.* Tubingen: Mohr, 1962–75.

Straus, Raphael. "The Jews in the Economic Evolution of Central Europe." *JSS* 3 (1941): 15–40.

Strauss, Herbert. "Liberalism and Conservatism in Prussian Legislation for Jewish Affairs, 1815–1847." *Curt C. Silberman Jubilee Volume,* edited by Herbert Strauss and Hanns Reissner, pp. 14–132. New York: American Federation of Jews from Central Europe, 1969.

————. "Pre-Emancipation Prussian Policies Towards the Jews, 1815–1847." *LBIY* 11 (1966): 107–36.

Swetchinski, Daniel M. "Kinship and Commerce: Foundations of Portuguese Jewish Life in Seventeenth Century Holland." *Studia Rosenthaliana* 15 (1981): 52–74.

Szajkowski, Zosa. *Autonomy and Communal Jewish Debts during the French Revolution of 1789.* New York, 1959.

————. *The Economic Status of the Jews in Alsace, Metz and Lorraine, 1648–1789.* New York: Editions Historiques Franco-Juives, 1954.

————. *Franco-Judaica.* New York: American Academy for Jewish Research, 1962.

————. "French Jews in the Armed Forces during the Revolution of 1789." *PAAJR* 26 (1957): 139–60.

————. "Internal Conflicts within the Eighteenth Century Sephardic Communities of France." *HUCA* 31 (1960): 167–80.

————. "Jewish Autonomy Debated and Attacked during the French Revolution." *HJ* 10 (1958): 31–46.

————. "The Jewish Problem in Alsace, Metz, and Lorraine on the Eve of the Revolution." *JQR* 44 (1953–54), 105–243.

————. "Jewish Religious Observance during the French Revolution of 1789." *YIVO Annual of Jewish Social Science* 12 (1958–59): 211–34.

————. *Jews and the French Revolutions of 1789, 1830 and 1848.* New York: Ktav Publishing House, 1970.

————. "Marriages, Mixed Marriages and Conversions among Jews during the Revolution of 1789." *HJ* 19 (1957): 33–54.

General Bibliography

──────. "Mishlahoteihem shel Yehudei Bordeaux el Va'adat Malesherbes ve-el ha-Aseifa ha-Le'umit." *Zion* 18 (1953): 31–79.

──────. "The Sephardic Jews of France during the Revolution of 1789." *PAAJR* 24 (1955): 137–64.

──────. "Synagogues during the French Revolution of 1789–1800." *JSS* 20 (1958): 215–29.

Talmon, Jacob L. *Romanticism and Revolt.* London: Thames and Hudson, 1973.

Tama, Diogene. *Actes du Grand Sanhedrin.* Paris, 1807.

──────. *Collection de procés-verbaux et decisions du Grand Sanhedrin.* Paris, 1807.

──────. *Proces-verbaux des seances de l'Assemblée des Deputés français professant la religion Juive.* Paris, 1807.

──────. *Transactions of the Parisian Sanhedrin.* Translated by F. D. Kirwan. London, 1807; rpr. Farnborough, 1971.

Toaf, Shabbatai. "Mahaloket Rabbi Ya'acov Sasportas u-Parnassei Livorno." *Sfunot* 9 (1965): 169–91.

Toland, John. *Reasons for Naturalizing the Jews of Great Britain and Ireland.* London, 1714. Rpr. Jerusalem: Hebrew University, Department of Jewish History, 1963.

"Toldot ha-Zman." *Ha-Measef,* pp. 331–34. Berlin, 1788.

Torat ha-Kena'ot. Amsterdam: D. Propos, 1845.

Wallach, Luitpold. "The Beginnings of the Science of Judaism in the Nineteenth Century." *HJ* 8 (1946): 33–60.

Wessely, Naphtali Herz. *Divrei Shalom ve-Emet.* Vienna: A. Shamir, 1826.

Wiener, Max. *ha-Dat ha-Yehudit be-Tekufat ha-Emancipazia.* Jerusalem: Mosad Bailik, 1974.

──────, ed. *Abraham Geiger and Liberal Judaism.* Translated by Ernst Schlochauer. Philadelphia: Jewish Publication Society, 1962.

Wolf, Immanuel. "On the Concepts of a Science of Judaism (1822)." Translated by Lionel E. Kochan. *LBIY* 2 (1957): 194–204.

Wolf, John B. *The Emergence of the Great Powers, 1685–1715.* New York: Harper, 1963.

Zimmerman, Sheldon. "Confronting the Halakha on Military Service." *Judaism* 20 (1971): 204–12.

Zinberg, Israel. *A History of Jewish Literature.* Vol. 8. Translated by B. Martin. New York: Ktav Publishing House, 1977.

Bibliography of
Talmudic Texts,
Classical Responsa, and
Rabbinic Commentaries

BT Avot

Beit ha-Behira (R. Menahem ha-Mei'iri, 1249–1316, Provençal scholar and commentator on the Talmud).

BT Bava Batra

BT Bava Kamma

BT Gittin

Haggahot Mordecai (fourteenth-century glosses by Samuel ben Aaron of Schlettstadt to the thirteenth-century code of Mordecai ben Hillel ben Hillel).

P.T. Hagiga

Hidushei ha-Ramban (Nahmanides, 1194–1270, Spanish Talmudist, exegete, and physician).

BT Ketubbot

Tosefta Ketubbot

BT Kiddushin

Likkutei She'elot u-Teshuvot Hatam Sofer (R. Moses Sofer, 1762–1829, leader of Orthodox Jewry, rabbi of Pressburg, 1806 until his death).

BT Nedarim

Pahad Yizhak (R. Isaac Hezekiah ben Samuel Lampronti, 1679–1756, Italian rabbi, physician, and educator).

Peirush ha-Mishnah (Maimonides, 1135–1204, Rabbinic authority and philosopher; born in Spain, Maimonides, known by the acronym Rambam, spent most of his adult life in Egypt, where he served as royal physician).

Piskei ha-Rosh (R. Asher ben Yeḥiel, ca. 1250–1327, Talmudist in France, Germany, and Spain).

B.T. Sanhedrin

Sefer ha-Tashbez (R. Simeon ben Ẓemaḥ Duran, ca. 1438–1510, rabbi and author, who spent most of his life in Algiers).

She'elot u-Teshuvot Darkhei Noam (R. Mordecai ha-Levi, seventeenth-century chief rabbi of Cairo).

She'elot u-Teshuvot Rabbi Akiva Eger (1761–1837, German rabbi).

She'elot u-Teshuvot Leḥem Rav (R. Abraham ben Moses di Boton, ca. 1545–88, Salonika-born rabbi and halakhist).

She'elot u-Teshuvot Maharam (R. Meir of Rothenburg, ca. 1215–93, German Talmudist, codifier, and liturgical poet).

She'elot u-Teshuvot Mahari Weil (R. Jacob ben Judah Weil, German rabbi and halakhic authority in the first half of the fifteenth century).

She'elot u-Teshuvot Maharik (R. Joseph Colon, ca. 1420–80, Italian halakhist).

She'elot u-Teshuvot Givat Pinḥas (R. Pinḥas Horowitz, ca. 1731–1805, German rabbi and Talmudic authority).

She'elot u Teshuvot ha-Radbaz (R. David ben Solomon ibn Zimra, 1479–1573, Spanish-born Talmudic scholar, halakhic authority, and kabbalist, who spent most of his life in Safed and Egypt).

She'elot u-Teshuvot ha-Ramban (Naḥmanides, 1194–1270, Spanish Talmudist, exegete, and physician).

She'elot u-Teshuvot Rashba (Solomon ben Abraham Adret, ca. 1235–1310, Spanish rabbi and one of the foremost Jewish scholars of his day).

She'elot u-Teshuvot ha-RI (ibn Migash, 1077–1141, greatest Spanish Talmudic scholar of the third generation of Spanish rabbis).

She'elot u-Teshuvot Ribash (R. Isaac ben Sheshet Perfet, 1326–1408, Spanish rabbi and halakhic authority).

Bibliography of Talmudic Texts and Commentaries

She'elot u-Teshuvot ha-Ritba (R. Yom Tov ben Abraham Asbili, ca. 1250–1330, Spanish Talmudist).

She'elot u-Teshuvot ha-Rosh (R. Asher ben Yeḥiel, ca. 1250–1327, Talmudist in France, Germany, and Spain.)

She'elot u-Teshuvot Ḥatam Sofer (R. Moses Sofer, 1762–1839, leader of Orthodox Jewry, rabbi of Pressburg, 1806 until his death).

She'elot u-Teshuvot Zera Emet (R. Ishmael of Modena, 1724–1811, Talmudic scholar and author.)

Shita Mekubbeẓet

Shulkhan Arukh (Joseph Caro, 1488–1575, born in Toledo, family moved to Portugal and later to Turkey; lived in Safed, 1536 until his death).

Terumat ha-Deshen (R. Israel Isserlein, foremost Talmudic authority of Germany in the first half of the fifteenth century).

PT Terumot

Teshuvah Me-Ahavah (R. Eliezer Fleckeles, 1754–1826, Austrian rabbi and author).

Tur (R. Jacob ben Asher, ca. 1270–1340, halakhic authority, born in Germany, lived in Toledo most of his adult life).

Yad ha-Ḥazzakah (Maimonides, 1135–1204).

BT Yevamot

Index

Index

About the Author. Gil Graff is Assistant Director of the Bureau of Jewish Education of Los Angeles and Adjunct Assistant Professor at the University of Judaism. He received his B.A. from Roosevelt University in Chicago and B.H.L. from Spertus College of Judaica. He has three M.A. degrees: in history from UCLA, in Jewish studies from the University of Judaism (Los Angeles), and in education from California State University. He received his Ph.D. and J.D. from UCLA. This is his first book.